DAT[...]

Zechariah

*Not yet published as of this printing.

BIBLE STUDY COMMENTARY

Zechariah

HOMER HEATER, JR.

Lamplighter Books
Grand Rapids, Michigan
Zondervan Publishing House

ZECHARIAH: BIBLE STUDY COMMENTARY

Lamplighter Books are published by the Zondervan Publishing House
1415 Lake Drive, S.E., Grand Rapids, Michigan 49506

Copyright © 1987 by Homer Heater, Jr.

Library of Congress Cataloging in Publication Data

Heater, Homer.
  Zechariah: Bible study commentary.

  (Bible study commentary series)
  1. Bible. O.T. Zechariah—Commentaries. I. Title. II. Series.
  BS1665.3.H43 1988   224'.9807   87-21624
  ISBN 0-310-36911-8

Edited by Nia Jones, John D. Sloan

Printed in the United States of America

87 88 89 90 91 / EP / 10 9 8 7 6 5 4 3 2 1

To my sons
Ken, Rick, Kevin, and John
"A wise son makes a father glad"

Contents

Introduction

A. The Importance of the Book of Zechariah

The importance of Zechariah is partially indicated by the number of times it is cited or alluded to in the New Testament. Zechariah is second only to Isaiah in frequency of citations in the passion narratives and has the greatest influence of all the prophets in John's apocalypse.

Yet Zechariah was also important to the Jews of the sixth century who had returned from the Exile. The destruction of the city and temple by Nebuchadnezzar in 586 B.C. had also destroyed the center of religious activity for God's people. Jeremiah's famous "temple sermon" (Jer. 7) shows that the people thought they were protected from God's judgment by the mere presence of the temple, regardless of their conduct. The loss of the temple was a shattering blow to that confidence.

The first eight chapters of Zechariah are directed to the reconstituted Jewish community and to the rebuilding of the temple. The seven "night visions" are encouraging messages to an isolated and apparently rejected people: They are not forgotten; the temple will be rebuilt! Further, there is an unimagined future for God's people. The many promises of a Davidic rule given by the pre-exilic and exilic prophets will indeed be fulfilled, but it will come through God's supernatural work in the midst of much tribulation and suffering (Zech. 9–14).

The temple is emphasized in Zechariah (as in Haggai).

Prophets prior to the Exile criticized the popular dependence on the temple as a religious symbol. They argued that a repentant heart was necessary for salvation. Further, temple sacrifices were only one part of the Jews' faith in God. Even so, the rebuilding of the temple was necessary (1) because of its close identification with Zion, God's chosen place, (2) because of the relationship between the temple and the covenant (the temple was a symbol of God's presence among the people), and (3) because of its eschatological implications: God's house would be established.[1]

Zechariah's significance to his contemporary Jews must be kept in mind to avoid a "proof-texting" of the various references to the Messiah. It was primarily a message for his day with obvious implications for a future day. That much of Zechariah is "apocalyptic" (full of symbols and unusual events) should not deter us from studying the book in detail for its meaning to the returned exiles and to us, who also look for the coming of the Messiah.

B. The Man Zechariah

The Hebrew name means "Jehovah remembers," a fitting name for a prophet whose message is full of reminders of Jehovah's faithfulness. When Zechariah is referred to in Ezra 5:1 and 6:14, he is called the son of Iddo; in the Book of Zechariah, as the son of Berekiah, son of Iddo. Nothing is known of a Berekiah, but Iddo is listed among the priests and Levites who accompanied Joshua and Zerubbabel from Babylon (Neh. 12:4). Zechariah may have been a priest, but since so many people in the Old Testament had that name, we cannot say dogmatically that he was a priest.[2]

C. The Historical Background of Zechariah

A momentous event occurred when Cyrus issued his famous edict permitting all religious groups to restore to their native lands the idols captured by Nebuchadnezzar. Cyrus was

---

[1] See Joyce Baldwin, *Haggai, Zechariah, Malachi* (Downers Grove, Ill.: InterVarsity Press, 1972), pp. 19–20.

[2] See Baldwin, *Haggai, Zechariah, Malachi*, p. 61, for her arguments that Zechariah was a priest.

fulfilling God's promises to return the Jews from their exile to Jerusalem (Isa. 45:1–13). The decree issued to the Jews is found in Ezra 1. The year was 538 B.C.

About 50,000 people made their way to Jerusalem under the leadership of Zerubbabel and Joshua the high priest. One of the first things they did was build an altar (Ezra 3:1–3). In the second year of their return (536 B.C.), they began construction on the temple (Ezra 3:8–13).

Rejected from participating in the worship of the Lord with the returning Jews, the Samaritans and other nonexiled Jews (probably worshipers of Jehovah in conjunction with other deities) caused enough trouble for the Jews that they were able to get an official order from the Persian government to stop the temple construction (Ezra 4:24). This order continued in effect for sixteen years until the second year of Darius (520 B.C.).

Under the urging of Haggai and Zechariah, Zerubbabel and Joshua resumed the work of building the temple (Ezra 5:1–2). Again, opposition arose, but this time the attempt to frustrate the work failed, and the temple was completed in 516 B.C.

The Book of Zechariah opens in the second year of Darius (520 B.C.), and the first six chapters deal with the state of the returned Jews. Chapters 7 and 8 take place two years later. Chapters 9–14 are undated, and their messages may have come to Zechariah years after the first eight chapters were given.

D. The Structure of the Book of Zechariah

Within critical studies, it has been popular to refer to at least three Zechariahs. Chapters 9–14 have been separated for reasons of style, vocabulary, and historical data from the first eight chapters. The contents of chapters 9–14 have been considered to be so fragmentary that no unified study is possible.[3]

A welcome trend in recent years has been the literary evaluation of the books of the Old Testament, stressing unity and forms instead of fragmentation. A significant work was presented in 1961 by P. Lamarche.[4] He argues that Zechariah

[3] See especially Baldwin, *Haggai, Zechariah, Malachi*, pp. 63–70, for a review of the history of exegesis of this book.

[4] P. Lamarche, *Zacharie IX–XIV, Structure Literaire et Messianisme* (Paris: Librairie LeCoffre, 1961).

9–14 has structural unity and that the material was contemporary with the sixth-century prophet. Baldwin, too, has applied the structural argument to the first eight chapters with good results.

The Book of Zechariah divides easily into two main parts. Chapters 1–8 contain visions and messages primarily concerned with the rebuilding of the temple and also speak of Israel's future; chapters 9–14 contain symbolic actions, predictions, and much material about eschatology (the study of last things). The second section divides again into two "burdens," defined as special prophetic messages, often negative in content, but not always. The first burden is in chapters 9–11 and speaks of victory over the Gentiles (9), prosperity for Israel (10), and the shepherd of Israel (11). The second burden is in chapters 12–14. This section speaks of salvation for Israel (12), sanctification of Israel (13), and the return of Israel's king (14).

Part I

Messages and Visions
The Rebuilding of the Temple
(Zechariah 1:1–8:23)

Chapter 1

Opening Message
(Zechariah 1:1–6)

The time of the opening message is the eighth month of the second year of Darius, King of Persia (520 B.C.). The Jews have been back in the land for seventeen or eighteen years.

The first message is a rebuke from the Lord. Zechariah says, "The LORD was very angry with your fathers" (1:2). This opening statement is designed to shake the theological memory of the returned exiles: "Remember the past." God's judgment, ever coupled with mercy, eventually comes to disobedient people, just as to the Jews in 586 B.C. when Nebuchadnezzar defeated King Zedekiah, destroyed the city and temple, and deported many Jews to Babylon.

The implications for this rebuke are found in 1:3: "Therefore, say to them, 'Thus says the LORD of hosts, Return to me . . . that I may return to you.'" The returnees had failed to learn the lessons of history. They were rebelling against the Lord, just as their ancestors had. The Lord was urging them to return to Him in repentance.

God sent prophets to Israel from the time they first entered the land to warn them about false gods and to encourage devotion to the one true God. The "former prophets" refer to those prophets from Joshua's time (c. 1400 B.C.) to the Exile (586 B.C.). The pre-exilic Jews consistently and persistently ignored God's warnings, and thus God's judgment came upon them. He admonishes them not to repeat the mistake of their ancestors.

The questions in 1:5 are a bit difficult. If they both come from Zechariah, they seem contradictory. "Where are your forefathers now?" (NIV) means that the Jews should remember that their forefathers were judged. The second question seems to imply that the prophets have disappeared also, and some commentaries suggest that the people retort with the second question. "If you say our fathers are gone because of disobedience, how do you account for the fact that the prophets are gone also?" However, Zechariah is saying that both the messengers (the prophets) and the recipients of the message (the fathers) are gone, but God's Word abides continually. The people are transient; God is eternal.

The proof of God's sovereignty is that His promises of judgment were fulfilled when their fathers went into captivity (1:6). Furthermore, the exiles were wise enough to recognize the hand of God and to repent. The latter part of 1:6 is a creedal statement hammered out on the anvil of affliction in Babylon. "The LORD Almighty has done to us what our ways and practices deserve, just as he has determined to do" (NIV).

The first message is to challenge the discouraged and despondent returnees to face up to their sin and the reality of God's work in their lives and turn to the One who can give them life. This argument sets the tone for the book and will be repeated later.

For Further Study

1. Zechariah is a book written for the returning exiles and contains much difficult material. Why should the believer today study it?

2. Read Jeremiah 7 and the book of Haggai. Evaluate the attitude of Jeremiah toward the temple and the attitude of the returned exiles.

3. Using a Bible dictionary, trace the history of the temple from Solomon's time to 70 A.D.

Chapter 2

Visions of God's Concern for His People
(Zechariah 1:7–2:13)

A. The First Vision: God's Watchful Care (1:7–17)

Three months after Zechariah's inaugural vision, God addresses the issue of Jerusalem's discomfort through a vision of horsemen.

1. The Characters (1:7–8)

At night Zechariah sees a man on a red horse standing among the myrtles in a low place. Behind that man are three horses: One is red; one, bright red; one, white. These have riders who speak in 1:11. Two more angels are introduced in 1:9–11. One is the angel "who was speaking with me." This angel helps Zechariah understand the visions. Commentators call him the interpreting angel. The Angel of the Lord appears in 1:11. Some identify the Angel of the Lord with the first rider of the vision who is also standing among the myrtle trees. Others think he is separate from the others. If he is a new character, there would be six personages altogether: three horsemen plus a fourth horseman who speaks first, the Angel of Jehovah, and the interpreting angel. While the phrase "Angel of Jehovah" does not always represent the second person of the Trinity, there are several places where it probably does, e.g., Judges 6 and 13, and it probably does here as well.

There are also horses in Revelation 6 whose colors are significant: The red horse stands for bloodshed; the black, for famine; the white, for victory. However, the passage in Revelation is quite different from Zechariah, and the angel does not identify the different colors in Zechariah. So these meanings should not be imposed on the colors here.

2. The Interpretation (1:9–12)

Zechariah, puzzled about the significance of the vision, turns to the interpreting angel and asks about it. The angel agrees to explain it. The man on the red horse (probably at the prompting of the interpreting angel) begins to explain the vision. He says that these horsemen have been sent by Jehovah to walk back and forth on the earth. The same Hebrew word is used in Job 1:7 and 2:2 to describe the way Satan investigates the world and makes reports to God.

Then the three other horsemen respond to the Angel of the Lord. Their report is that all the land is at rest and quiet. In his second year Darius was consolidating the Persian Empire, and so all the land was at rest. Olmstead states that by this time Darius had made much progress in establishing his rule and putting down all resistance.[1] This quietness should not be a problem. Surely, peace in the world is good for Israel, but the Angel of Jehovah explains the problem by crying out, "O, LORD of hosts, how long wilt thou have no compassion for Jerusalem and the cities of Judah, with which thou hast been indignant these seventy years?"

The seventy-year period referred to is the time of God's judgment upon His people. This period was first predicted in Jeremiah 25:11. Daniel believed it was coming to a conclusion when he prayed to the Lord (9:2), but according to the Angel's statement, it has not yet ended, in spite of the fact that the Jews had returned from the Exile.

The beginning of the seventy-year period cannot be computed from Nebuchadnezzar's first attack against Jerusalem in 605 B.C. because that battle was already past when Jeremiah made the prediction. It should be computed from the destruction of the temple in 586 B.C. God's judgment is viewed as continuing while the temple lies unfinished. The meaning of the vision of the horsemen is that Israel is still in trouble. The

---

[1] A. T. Olmstead, *History of the Persian Empire* (Chicago: University of Chicago Press, 1923), pp. 135–144.

city lies in ruins, the temple is yet to be completed, and the organization of the people is weak. At the same time, the Gentiles, who know not God, seem to be doing quite well. The age-old question is asked, "Why, God, do you let such situations exist?"

3. God's Promise (1:13–17)

Jehovah Himself responds to the plaintive cry of the Angel of Jehovah, but He speaks to the interpreting angel since the message is really for Zechariah. His words are "good" and "comforting." Their content is given in the following verses.

Zechariah is told to proclaim that God has two attitudes. First, He is jealous for Jerusalem and Zion. Jealousy on God's part represents a strong, protective attitude that includes discipline where necessary. God has had a "great jealousy" for Jerusalem and Zion (Jerusalem and Zion are to be equated). In His jealousy, He punished them for their rejection of Jehovah, and thus they are now in disarray. The statement of 1:15 is an important theological issue in the Old Testament. God had used the Gentile nations to punish Israel, but they exceeded their mandate and became arrogant toward Israel. Therefore, God is angry at the Gentiles who are now at peace while Israel suffers. This brings Him to the heart of His promise (16–17).

God's second attitude is one of mercy toward His people. "Therefore, thus says the LORD" is an opening statement of a prophecy (literally, "Therefore, thus has Jehovah said. . . ."). The promise is that God will return to Jerusalem in mercy. According to the Hebrew verb tense used, "I will return" means the act is already accomplished as far as God is concerned. The word *compassion* is plural, probably to show the many facets of God's compassion. Furthermore, the house of God (the temple) will be built and the city as well (the stretched-out line is an architect's measuring line). This, then, is a promise that the temple will be completed and the city will be rebuilt. The temple was completed in 516 B.C., and the walls were built by Nehemiah some sixty years after that.

Zechariah is told to cry out the second time and expand this promise of God (1:17). The strong introductory statement, "Thus says the LORD of hosts," is again given. "My cities [not only

Jerusalem] will again overflow with prosperity" because of God's blessing upon them. Furthermore, He will "again comfort Zion and again choose Jerusalem."

4. Summary

This vision was designed to encourage the Jews and their leaders. God was fully aware of the dismal state of affairs in which His people found themselves. He was in charge of the world, however much it seemed otherwise, and His purposes for Jerusalem and Judah would yet be fulfilled.

Many of the prophecies of Zechariah reach down to a future time, but this one applies to the period of 520 B.C. and immediately following. God promises that the temple and city will be rebuilt, and they were.

God's children in every age should be encouraged by the fact that God has His messengers checking up on the world and working in it. It is not always evident that God is in charge, for the evil elements so often prevail, but God will always vindicate Himself and His people.

B. The Second Vision: Four Horns, Four Craftsmen—God's Vindication (1:18–21)

The first vision shows God's concern for the suffering of Judah while her enemies prosper. He concludes that vision with a promise to rebuild the temple and to bring great blessing on Jerusalem. The second vision takes up the same theme.

1. The Four Horns (1:18–19)

The phrase "Then I lifted up my eyes and behold . . ." is similar to the phrase in 1:8: "I saw at night and behold . . ." These two phrases link this section with the first vision. A new facet of the encouragement of God is about to be given.

Zechariah sees in a vision four horns and asks the interpreting angel to explain them to him. The interpreting angel says that the four horns represent those who have scattered Judah, Israel, and Jerusalem. The word translated *scattered* is in an intensive form depicting a violent action.

It is clear from 1:21 that the four horns represent nations. The horn is a symbol of power and is often applied to nations.

The tribe of Joseph is described as having the horns of a wild ox (Deut. 33:17). Hannah, in speaking of God's blessings on her, says that her horn is high (1 Sam. 2:1). She also says that God will exalt the horn of His anointed (1 Sam. 2:10). The defeat of Moab is described as cutting off her horns (Jer. 48:25). The horns of the brazen altar and altar of incense were probably to depict God's power (Exod. 27:2; 30:2). Daniel puts special emphasis on the horns in the eighth chapter of his prophecy where they clearly represent nations.

Specifically, these four horns represent nations that have scattered Judah, Israel, and Jerusalem. The difficulty is determining which particular nations. It was Assyria who took Israel into captivity (2 Kings 17:1–6), and Judah was removed by the Babylonians (2 Kings 25:1–12). However, no other two nations in ancient history seem to fit this role. Persia cannot be said to have scattered the Jews; on the contrary, they restored the Jews to their land.

Some commentators identify the four horns with the four kingdoms of Daniel 2 and 7, but the same problems exist, especially since Zechariah's vision is directed primarily to Israel of the restoration. Therefore, the four horns should be understood in a general way as powers coming from the four quarters of the earth. (God promises to regather Israel from the four quarters of the earth, Isa. 11:12.) The four horns represent any and all nations that have scattered Israel and Judah.

2. *The Four Craftsmen (1:20–21)*

The Lord then showed Zechariah four craftsmen. When Zechariah asks the meaning of the four craftsmen, he is reminded again of the four horns and told that the four craftsmen have the task of throwing down the four horns. The Hebrew word translated "craftsman" is a general term for any kind of a skilled worker, whether in stone, wood, or metal, so there is no way to know what type of craftsman is meant. The fact that they are to "throw down" the horns may indicate that they have saws with which they are going to cut them off and then throw them down.

Zechariah does not ask who the four craftsmen are. He wants to know what they are going to do, for he sees them coming with tools in their hand (1:21). The interpreting angel explains that the craftsmen have come to terrify and throw down the horns of the nations who have been guilty of scattering Israel.

The oppression of Judah by the four horns is further described in 1:21 with the phrase, "so that no man lifts up his head." The devastation of Judah is so complete that none dares raise his head. The word *terrify* means literally "to cause to tremble." God will bring all nations into obedience and fear (cf. Psalm 2).

The four craftsmen correspond to the four horns. Since the four horns represent nations from all quarters of the earth, the four craftsmen represent those nations that God will raise up to judge those who punished Israel.

The clear message is that no matter how dismal the present seems, no matter that unbelieving nations appear to be in control of human events, God will still deliver Israel.

3. Summary

God acknowledged through this vision that His people Israel were in a defeated state because of surrounding nations. He promised to vindicate Israel by judging those nations through other nations. The fulfillment of this promise has not yet happened, and Israel is certainly not free from threats on every side. During the Great Tribulation (Rev. 6–19), Israel will be the special target of Antichrist's wrath. Even then, God promises to protect her (Rev. 12). It will be then and only then that these promises will be ultimately fulfilled.

It is significant that Zechariah *sees* the four horns (the problem), but the Lord has to *show* him the four craftsmen (the solution). God is gently but firmly pointing out to Zechariah that He is in charge and will deal with Israel's problems. How often does the believer see only the problems until God graciously points out that He will turn even painful events into the believer's good.

C. The Third Vision: The Measuring Line—Jerusalem Will Be Rebuilt (2:1–13)

God promises future prosperity for Jerusalem in 1:17. This third vision assures that promise under the symbol of a measuring line.

1. The Man with the Measuring Line (2:1–2)

Zechariah lifted up his eyes and saw the next vision (cf. 1:8, 18). What he saw was a man with a measuring line who told Zechariah that he was going to measure Jerusalem. The word translated "line" is the same as that in Psalm 16:6: "The lines have fallen to me in pleasant places; indeed my heritage is beautiful to me." Zechariah has already been told that a measuring line would be stretched over Jerusalem, when the Lord says, "I will return to Jerusalem with compassion; My house will be built in it" (1:16). Therefore, the measuring line indicates that God is going to build Jerusalem.

There is a strikingly similar passage in Ezekiel 40:3, where we see a man with a cord and a measuring rod in his hand. He also measures the city and temple, that is, the temple to be built during the Millennium. The description of the man in Ezekiel suggests a heavenly personage, and since he is referred to as Jehovah in 44:2, 5, he may be the Angel of Jehovah. Likewise, the man in Zechariah's vision may well be the Angel of Jehovah (he speaks as Jehovah in 2:5).

2. The Message of the Messengers (2:3–5)

The interpreting angel approaches the man with the measuring line to see what is about to happen. A third character now appears. He is called "another angel," and he goes out to meet the interpreting angel. This "other angel" speaks to the interpreting angel and gives him a message for Zechariah ("that young man"). The message must be urgent, for he tells the interpreting angel to run to tell Zechariah.

a. Jerusalem will be unwalled and yet fully inhabited (2:4)
The angel tells Zechariah that there will be a large population of people and animals in Jerusalem and that the city will not have walls, even though Jerusalem is one of the most famous walled

cities in history. (At this time, the Turkish walls from the
fifteenth century A.D. provide a graphic illustration of an ancient
walled city.) Jerusalem will be unwalled because the number of
people and cattle will be so large that a walled city could not
contain them.

   b. Jerusalem's protection (2:5). The whole purpose of a wall
is for protection. If Jerusalem lies as an unwalled city, she will
be vulnerable to attack. The answer to that problem is in 2:5:
"For I," declares the Lord, "will be a wall of fire around her,
and I will be the glory in her midst." God declares that He
Himself will be a protective wall of fire around the city. The
construction is very emphatic: God is interposing Himself
between His people and her enemies.

   c. The glory of Jehovah (2:5). He will also be her glory
within her. This future glory is like Israel's wilderness experi-
ence when God manifested Himself to her and led her by a
cloud and a pillar of fire. This glory may also indicate that the
shekinah glory of God that departed from the temple in
Ezekiel's vision (Ezek. 10:18–19) has returned to the city and
the temple.

   The fulfillment of this prophecy does not take place in
Zechariah's time, but there is much debate as to when it will be
fulfilled. Many of the older commentaries insist that this vision
must be a metaphor for the church because they cannot accept a
literal future for Israel. However, reading Zechariah leads to the
conclusion that a time is coming when God will restore Israel to
a place of blessing and prosperity in the Millennium.

3. The Regathering of Israel (2:6–9)

   The vision uses a prophetic word to explain how the events
of 2:4–5 will take place.

   a. The warning to flee the land of the north (2:6). The reason
the Jews are warned to flee from the land of the north is that
judgment is coming to those nations that have despoiled Israel.
Geographically, any people attacking Israel (except for Egypt)
came from the north, since coming from the east would require
crossing the desert. So the people of Assyria and Babylonia had
to travel north by means of the fertile crescent and attack from
Lebanon or Syria.

b. The warning to flee Babylonia (2:7). The district is made more specific in 2:7 when Babylonia is mentioned. Having been conquered by Cyrus in 539 B.C., Babylonia in Zechariah's day was no longer a national power. However, Jews were still living in that area, and now they are warned to flee because Babylonia and all her successors will be judged. It would be better to be out of those nations when that happens.

c. The sent one (2:8). The eighth verse is very significant. The Lord of hosts is speaking, but the one to whom He is speaking is acting in the capacity of Jehovah. He is to regather Israel, a task only Jehovah can do. Hence, Jehovah is sending Jehovah! This mysterious statement is a foreshadowing of the coming of God in flesh (John 1:14).

The clause in 2:8 "after glory he has sent me" is not clear. Most commentators take it to mean "for the purpose of setting forth God's glory." They may be correct, but the word translated "after" does not usually have this meaning. In any event, God will judge the nations who are now abusing Israel. The special place Israel has in God's plan is illustrated by the phrase "apple of his eye." This expression refers to the pupil of the eye and, therefore, to something very dear and precious to its owner. Israel holds such a favored position with God, and woe to those who try to despoil her.

d. The regathering of Israel (2:9). The time is coming when the "sent one" will wave His hand over the nations and their own slaves will turn on them (2:9). When all this takes place, Israel will recognize the divine commission of the "sent one." The Jews, according to 2:6, were scattered to the four winds of heaven. In Zechariah's day, the Jews had been deported primarily to southern Mesopotamia. In subsequent scatterings (Hellenistic and Roman), they were spread out literally to the four winds. Although a small group of Jews returned in Zechariah's day, and many have returned in modern times, the great regathering of Israel is yet to come.

4. The Indwelling of Israel (2:10–13)

God tells Israel to be happy and to rejoice for He will dwell in Zion's midst. A recurring theme in the Old Testament is that Jehovah will be Israel's God, and they will be His people.

Furthermore, the blessing will extend to the nations who will join themselves to Israel (Rom. 11:15). All of this will vindicate the "sent one." At that time God will possess Judah as His portion and will choose Jerusalem again.

None of these marvelous promises have yet been fulfilled in Israel. Since it is improper to violate a literal interpretation to make it apply to the church, the only option left is that these events await a future fulfillment in the Millennium.

In the presence of this magnificent prophecy, all humanity must sit in hushed awe before the Lord (2:13). When God is stirred from His holy dwelling, people must stand aside and see the glory of God.

5. Summary

The third vision reveals God's loving protection of His holy people and His holy city. Jerusalem will be restored; Israel will be regathered from the four quarters of the earth; the land will be prosperous; and, best of all, God will dwell in the midst of His people manifesting His shekinah glory.

The interpretation of this vision applies to the future, restored Israel. Then God will dwell in the midst of His people Israel, but in the present, He dwells in His church (1 Cor. 3:16). What a blessing that the holy, sovereign God would stoop to indwell sinful humanity. The church also should sit in hushed silence before His wonderful, gracious presence.

For Further Study

1. What is the basic meaning of the vision of the horsemen and what are the implications of that for the believer today?

2. The angel speaks of seventy years in 1:12. Read Jeremiah 25 and 29 and explain the significance of this number.

3. Compare the vision of the horns and craftsmen with Isaiah 10:5–19 and explain God's use of nations in the Old Testament.

4. Look up "measuring line" in a Bible dictionary and explain its significance in this context.

Chapter 3

Visions of Cleansing and Service
(Zechariah 3:1–5:11)

A. The Fourth Vision: The Cleansing of Israel (3:1–10)

The first three visions dealt with the provision of God for His people Israel. In spite of their dilemma, He promised a future time of blessing. The dilemma was caused by Israel's sin, but nothing was said about how the sin question was to be solved. The vision of chapter 3 deals with that question. Though the person of the vision is an individual, it is clear that he stands for the people because he is not personally charged in 3:9, where it is the impurity of the *land* that is being removed. Consequently, the question confronted in this chapter is how sinful Israel can stand before a holy God. A further question asks how the priesthood, so corrupt before the Exile, can be restored (cf. Ezek. 21:26–27).

The full blessing of God cannot come upon Israel through the rebuilding of the temple, but through God's redemptive work. This redemptive work will be carried out through the coming Servant of Jehovah (cf. Isa. 53), the Branch (Zech. 3:8; 6:12), who is symbolically represented by Joshua the high priest in 3:1–7.

1. The Defendant (3:1)

It is the Lord Himself, not the interpreting angel, who shows Zechariah this vision. The first person to appear is Joshua the high priest (whose name means "Jehovah saves"). Some believe this scene takes place in the temple or at the city gate (in a vision), but Zechariah probably sees it in the heavenly court as in Job 1 and 1 Kings 22:19–22. In both accounts, God is sitting on a throne surrounded by heavenly beings, and in Job's case, the messengers of God are going back and forth and Satan is accusing Job before his Benefactor.

Levitical instruction teaches that the high priest stands in place of the people before God (cf. the Day of Atonement ministry, Lev. 16). Therefore, it is unnecessary to look for some specific sins of Joshua for which he is being accused. He stands for the nation, much as Daniel identifies with the people in Daniel 9.

The two great personages in this book are Joshua, the high priest, and Zerubbabel, the governor. But it would be wrong to presume that the thrust of this prophecy is exhausted in these two men. The scope of Zechariah's message goes beyond their time.

2. The Judge/Defender (3:1)

Joshua is standing before the Angel of Jehovah. To stand before someone in Hebrew often means to serve him (cf. 1 Sam. 16:21). Joshua is serving in the courts of Jehovah before the Angel of Jehovah. As already noted, the Angel of Jehovah in the Old Testament often represents deity (cf. Judg. 6 and 13), and in this chapter, the Angel of Jehovah is Jehovah Himself, who speaks in 3:2. Here the critics add "angel" to avoid the clear implications of the text (i.e., that the angel is Jehovah), but no such addition is needed. God has revealed Himself to Zechariah through the Angel of Jehovah who is Jehovah.

3. The Prosecutor (3:1)

Satan is standing at the right hand of Joshua to accuse him. The word *Satan* is a transliteration of the Hebrew word "to accuse." The definite article is also used—*the* Satan, *the* great accuser. (The Septuagint translates this word *Diabolos* from which comes the word *Devil*.) The scene is complete. Joshua represents the priesthood and the people of Israel, and Satan is there to show them that they are worthy of God's judgment. This chapter provides early insight into the workings of the Evil One who has made it his task to "accuse the brethren" before God

(Rev. 12:10). Satan's battle is against God, but his attack is directed at God's chosen ones, whether Israel in the Old Testament or the church in the New Testament.

4. The Defense (3:2)

The content of the accusation is not given. Job 1:9, 10 and 2:4, 5 give examples of the types of accusation Satan makes against God's chosen ones. Whatever the accusation, Satan is cut off by the rebuke of the Lord Himself. The word *to rebuke* indicates more than a mild reproof; it is used with the meaning of "to forbid" (cf. Mal. 3:11; Ps. 106:9). Satan is not permitted to say more against Joshua as the representative of God's people.

This fact is emphasized by the additional statement, "The LORD who has chosen Jerusalem rebuke you." The elect position of Israel is stressed. Satan is unable to bring charges against Israel even though she deserves them because God has chosen her. This statement is reminiscent of Romans 8:33, "Who will bring a charge against God's elect? God is the one who justifies."

God's redemptive work is further emphasized by the question, "Is this not a brand plucked from the fire?" This metaphor is used in Amos 4:11: "and you were like a firebrand snatched [delivered] from a blaze." Israel is in desperate straits—barely snatched from the fire—yet God's grace is shown when he delivers her. No one deserves redemption. All are the object of God's consuming wrath, but by His matchless grace, Israel is "plucked from the fire" and stands in God's grace.

5. The Guilt of the Defendant (3:3–5)

It is only after the strong, irrefutable defense by God, who acts both as defense attorney (1 John 2:1) and as judge, that attention is turned to the guilt of the defendant. Whatever Satan said about the priesthood and Israel was probably true, just as it is in the case of believers today. Since Joshua (Israel) stands before the Angel of Jehovah and is unfit to be there, something must be done, and thus the Angel of Jehovah in 3:4 turns to the filthy garments. He orders those angels standing before Him to remove the garments. Lest there be any confusion as to the meaning of this symbolic action, the Angel says, "See, I have taken your iniquity away from you and will clothe you with festal robes." The only way Israel's sins could be removed and the priesthood be cleansed was by a supernatural act of God. The new garments (the word translated *garments* is used only here and in Isa. 3:22) represent imputed righteousness, that is, undeserved righteousness "put on the believer's account." The imputation of Christ's righteousness is only fully revealed in the New Testament, but it is implicit here in this act of reclothing. The same metaphor occurs in Paul's writings in which the believer has divested himself of the old life and is enjoined to put on the new man (Col. 3:9–11).

At this point (3:5), Zechariah bursts out with the request that Joshua be given a clean tiara. The tiara (miter) is the head covering or turban worn by the high priest, as described in Exodus 28:4, 37, 39. On it was attached the plate of pure gold engraved with the phrase "Holy to the LORD." The high priest represented God to the people and the people to God, so his office was particularly holy. The filthy garments are replaced with festal robes, signifying purification before God. The continued presence of the dirty turban would have indicated that the high priest was unfit to serve; however, the clean turban now qualifies the priest to function in the ministry of God. Therefore, Israel as a people must be made clean to come into the presence of God and to serve Him. Since Israel has sinned and has been punished by the Exile, her sins must be cleansed in order to restore the people and the priests to favor and service.

During all the time Joshua is being reclothed, the Angel of the Lord is supervising the activity to assure that it will be carried out properly. As the preincarnate Christ, He is responsible for the cleansing of those who come to God and become His servants.

6. The Promise (3:6–7)

The Angel of Jehovah now speaks solemnly to Joshua. The word *admonished* is a judicial term, meaning "to call as witness," so the promise that follows is a very serious statement. It refers to the reinstatement of the priesthood disrupted during the Exile. God is calling upon Joshua, his successors, and all Israel to recognize the importance of the priesthood and the purity demanded of that priesthood.

The promise is introduced by "thus says the LORD of hosts" (3:7). This phrase is often used by the prophets to indicate that a strong statement is being made by God. Lord of hosts is a title indicating God's sovereign control of the activities of the universe. What He is about to promise, He is able to carry out. The promise to Joshua is a conditional one. "If you will walk in My ways, and if you will perform My service . . ." These are concepts that could be applied to the entire nation, but the rest of the conditional sentence indicates that they are limited to the priesthood. It is a statement to Joshua and those who succeed him in the priesthood. "To walk in God's ways" is to obey His Word and to live a life conditioned by God's instruction. "Performing the service" refers sometimes to obeying God's Word in general but here probably refers to the priests' duties in the temple. Personal holiness and official competency are therefore the conditions of the promise about to be given.

If the conditions are met, then Joshua will be permitted full control of the temple duties. The construction is emphatic: "You will indeed be permitted to govern My house and also have charge of My courts." To govern God's house means to rule and supervise the temple of God; to have charge of the courts, which include the external areas of the sanctuary, is almost synonymous. God is therefore promising Joshua and his successors the right to direct and serve in the temple of God if their personal conduct is what it should be.

The third part of the promise is obscure. The Hebrew word translated *free access* appears as a plural only here. The singular form of the word means a "journey" or "walk" as in Jonah 3:3. Although there are different interpretations, understanding it to mean access to God is the best one. As the angels have been walking "to and fro" on the earth (1:11; Job 1:7) and then presenting themselves to God (Job 1:6), so Joshua the high priest and his successors are promised access to God. Through their intercessory ministries, they will have access in the same way as the angels ("these who are standing here").

7. The Coming Branch (3:8–10)

Joshua and his fellow priests are now admonished to pay careful attention to what God is about to say (3:8). "Your friends" refers to the other members of the priesthood serving under Joshua. God says that Joshua and his companions are to be considered signs or symbols. The word translated *symbol* sometimes refers to a miraculous event (Exod. 7:9) and sometimes simply means a symbol (cf. Isaiah's sons, Isa. 8:18). Here it means a symbol.

So the priesthood and the removing of the filthy garments from Joshua are symbolic. What they symbolize is explained in the rest of 3:8: "For behold, I am going to bring in My servant the Branch." This verse represents a very important theological concept. God's cleansing of Joshua is a symbolic act of His cleansing of the nation of Israel, but the cleansing must take place through the coming Branch who is symbolized by the priests. The Branch has a priestly work to perform.

The identity of this Branch is very important. Some say the Branch is Zerubbabel (because of Zech. 6:12, to be discussed later), but Zerubbabel is already on the scene, whereas the Branch is yet to come. The early Jewish interpretation, which was developed because of other Scriptures, was that the Branch referred to the Messiah. (The Jewish Aramaic Targum in 6:12 has "messiah.") Isaiah 4:2 says: "In that day the Branch of the LORD will be beautiful and glorious." This verse is found in a millennial context along with the washing away of the filth of the daughters of Zion (4:4). Jeremiah uses the word *Branch* in clearly messianic contexts (23:5, 6 and 33:15). The same imagery is being used here. Isaiah 11:1 and 53:2 use different words for branch, but the contexts are clearly messianic. Add to this the use of "My Servant" as a messianic title from Isaiah, and the passage yields a clear prediction of the coming Messiah. He is coming to cleanse His people.

The most difficult part of this section is 3:9. There is a stone with seven eyes and an engraving on it. It must have something to do with the cleansing of Israel because of the clause that follows it: "And I will remove the iniquity of that land." Since there is little agreement on the meaning of this verse, dogmatism must be avoided in its interpretation. The stone may well be another designation of the Messiah, as many in the church have held (cf. Ps. 118:22; Isa. 8:14 with Matt. 21:42 and 1 Peter 2:6). The seven eyes may represent God's watchful care over the Messiah. As to the engraving, it would be sheer speculation to try to identify it. It may indeed represent something like "the holiness of God" or "precious," but since God has not chosen to reveal its meaning, there is no way to know.

The most significant part of the vision is not couched in symbol. God states that He will remove the iniquity of that land in one day. Iniquity under the symbol of filth is the subject of this chapter and pertains to the cleansing of Israel's sin. The meaning of the "one day" is crucial. Certainly, the Crucifixion is the one act of God by which He forever dealt with sin, but the application to national Israel is left for another time. Paul, in that great prophetic eleventh chapter of Romans, says, "And thus all Israel will be saved; just as it is written, 'The deliverer will come from Zion, He will remove ungodliness from Jacob. And this is My covenant with them, when I take away their sins'" (vv. 26–27). There is a day coming in which "every eye will see Him, even those who pierced Him" (Rev. 1:7). God will then remove Israel's sin.

8. Summary

Israel has returned from the Exile, but the temple remains unbuilt and Israel remains uncleansed. This chapter predicts the cleansing of Israel through the coming of the Messiah and the millennial age to follow when everyone will invite his neighbor to sit under his vine and fig tree.

In the New Testament, the redeemed of the church are called a royal priesthood (1 Peter 2:9). They have been cleansed positionally (John 13:10) and may therefore act as priests coming "with confidence to the throne of grace" (Heb. 4:16). The church should rejoice in their priestly position and use that position to intercede for themselves and for others.

B. The Fifth Vision: God's Power (4:1–14)

The fifth vision of the night addresses the problem of rebuilding of the temple. As already noted, the once promising task of rebuilding the temple has come to a stop. God is using Haggai and Zechariah to get the people involved in the work. Haggai challenges the people on a personal level to get busy building the temple: "Consider your ways! Go up to the mountains, bring wood and rebuild the temple, that I may be pleased with it and be glorified,' says the LORD" (Hag. 1:7–8). The message to Zechariah concerns the same problem, but in this vision God's ability is stressed. Although the opposition from non-Jews and the apathy of the Jews resulted in the cessation of the work, the vision of the lampstand shows how this formidable task is to be accomplished.

1. The Vision (4:1–3)

The interpreting angel arouses Zechariah from a trancelike state to show him this new vision (4:1). In his typical, pedagogical fashion, he asks Zechariah what he sees. Zechariah, drawn from his reverie, peers into the vision and describes what he sees.

a. The Lampstand (4:2). The first thing he describes is a lampstand. The lampstand in the tabernacle is referred to twenty-five times. The lampstands in the temple are mentioned nine times (e.g., 1 Kings 7:49). Only once (2 Kings 4:10) is "lampstand" used in a nonsacred sense. Therefore, in this chapter the lampstand most likely refers to the lampstand of the temple.

The lampstand is chosen to represent the work of the temple probably because special provision was necessary for it to function. The oil for the lampstand was provided under the supervision of the priest from a central container to illustrate divine providence (Num. 4:16). This concept will be developed later.

b. The Bowl (4:2). There was a bowl on top of the lampstand. The word *bowl* is used for any liquid container. Zechariah's vision has a large bowl above the lampstand as the source of oil for each lamp. In the tabernacle, the oil was supplied by hand to each lamp on the lampstand (Exod. 25:6, 31–40).

c. The Lamps (4:2). As in the tabernacle (Exod. 25:37), there are seven lamps on this lampstand, each having connecting pipes to the bowl. The Hebrew uses an idiom to express the idea of seven pipes, one to each of the seven lamps.

d. The Olive Trees (4:3). Standing on either side of the bowl was an olive tree. The olive tree was famous as a source of oil. These two trees are the source of the oil for the lamps in Zechariah's vision.

2. The General Interpretation of the Vision (4:4–10)

Zechariah asks about the significance of the vision. The angel responds with a rhetorical question: "Do you not know what these are?" (The Hebrew stresses the word *these.*) This question is a device to bring attention to the importance of the subject by creating suspense. Zechariah replies politely, "No, my lord," and the interpreting angel proceeds to give the import of the vision.

a. The Temple/Tabernacle Lampstand. Since the background of the vision is the temple/tabernacle lampstand, it should be helpful to examine its importance for worship. The significance of the lampstand is not given anywhere in the Old Testament; however, the lampstand must have had considerable significance, since the priests trimmed the wicks daily, filled each lamp with specially made oil, and kept it burning in the holy place of the tabernacle. The symbolism of light is used extensively in Scripture, especially in Job, Psalms, and Isaiah; for example, "thy word is a lamp to my feet" (Ps. 119:105). Using the lampstand to represent the light of God's truth to and through Israel, Paul reminds the Philippian Christians that they are "light holders" (Phil. 2:15), and the seven churches of Revelation 2–3 are symbolized by the lampstands.

b. The Meaning of God's Work (4:6). The Word of the Lord is now directed to Zerubbabel through the interpreting angel. The message is that God's work in the world is not to be accomplished by might or power, but by God's Spirit. The word *power* in Hebrew is a word used generally for strength, might, or power, but the word translated *might* has a wider range of meanings. It refers to wealth, or an army, or a valiant person, even a virtuous person.

c. The Purpose of God's Strength. The intent of this statement is to encourage Zerubbabel who was facing a formi-

dable task. The opposition of the enemies and the apathy of the
Jews made the task of completing the temple almost impossible.
The message to Zerubbabel is that the task will not be
completed by sheer human effort. Whatever the human resources available—strength, authority, or wealth—they would
be insufficient for the task. The little word *but* in 4:6 is a strong
adversative in Hebrew and draws a contrast between human
resources and God's ability. This temple would be completed
only as God provided the resources.

d. **The Removal of the Opposition (4:7).** The message
continues more explicitly in 4:7: "What are you, O great
mountain?" This great mountain represents difficulty in completing the temple. Some believe it refers to a world power, and
the Persian government did indeed stop the work of the temple
at first (Ezra 4) but subsequently allowed it to continue (Ezra 5).
It should probably be construed as the general obstacles to the
completion of the task. Whatever it is, before Zerubbabel it will
become as a level place. The result of the Spirit's work will be
that Zerubbabel will bring out the head stone (the cap stone)
accompanied with shouts of approval, which indicates that the
temple will be finished.

e. **The Completion of the Temple (4:8–9).** God becomes
even more explicit in verses eight and nine. Zerubbabel has laid
the foundation stone (Ezra 3:8), and he will complete it. The
next phrase in 4:9, "Then you will know that the LORD of hosts
has sent me to you," occurs in 2:9, 11 and 6:15. Just as in other
references, the person being sent here is the Angel of Jehovah.
God's divine activity will be authenticated when His promised
work is completed.

f. **God's Method (4:10).** The final phrase of the interpretation (4:10) is the most difficult. "For who has despised the day of
small things?" probably means "who *ever* despises small
things?" That is, all great things must begin with small things.[1]
Zerubbabel's temple was small when compared with Solomon's
temple, and the old men wept at the small foundation (Ezra
3:12); however, God's work in Israel will be great. Some will

---

[1] So writes Carl F. Keil, "Zechariah," vol. 2 of *Biblical Commentary on the
Old Testament*, trans. by James Martin (Grand Rapids: Eerdmans, 1951), pp.
273–74.

rejoice when they see the plummet in Zerubbabel's hand. (The plummet is a symbol of building activity—an instrument used to assure that the walls are straight.) Those who will rejoice are the seven eyes on the engraved stone mentioned first in 3:9 as looking; here as going back and forth in all the earth. The same language was used in 1:10 of the horsemen who are investigating all the earth, likewise the same Hebrew word is used in 2 Chronicles 16:9 where the eyes of the Lord are going back and forth in the earth to support those whose heart is right. Therefore, God is keeping an eye on His work and will see that it is done.

3. Further Interpretative Questions (4:11–14)

Zechariah is not yet satisfied. He asks for an explanation of the two olive trees standing on the right and left of the lampstand. Before the angel responds, Zechariah then asks for an explanation of the two branches of the olive trees that are on the right and left of the lampstand and the two golden pipes through which the golden oil is flowing. This questioning leads to additional information. Each of the olive trees has a fruitful branch that is pouring oil through two golden pipes into the bowl and from there into the lamps.

a. The Angel's Interpretation (4:13–14). The interpreting angel increases the suspense by again implying that Zechariah should know what these represent (4:13). He then explains. These two olive trees represent the two anointed ones (Hebrew, "sons of oil") who stand before the Lord of all the earth. He does not explain who the two anointed ones are. Many suggestions have been made, but the most obvious is that they represent the two outstanding men in this book and period of time: Joshua the high priest, representing the religious authority, and Zerubbabel, representing the civil authority. The nation of Israel had both a civil office (the king) and a religious office (the priesthood). Both were considered to be spiritual offices in the theocratic kingdom. In this vision, Joshua and Zerubbabel are the two people through whom God is working to carry out His divine will. Those two offices have been combined in the Messiah (cf. Heb. 7).

b. Revelation 11. Since there is an allusion to Zechariah 4 in

Revelation 11:1–14, the two chapters need to be compared. The temple is being measured in 11:1–3. Then authority is given to God's two witnesses who will prophecy 1,260 days clothed in sackcloth (11:3). The allusion to Zechariah 4 is made in 11:4. The two witnesses "are the two olive trees and the two lampstands that stand before the LORD of the earth."

Much of the imagery of the Book of Revelation comes from Zechariah. However, similar imagery does not necessitate the same interpretation. Zechariah speaks of building the temple through two men who are divinely empowered. In the Tribulation, the temple will be built, and two men will bear witness of God. There the similarity ends. Each of the two passages has its own meaning: Zechariah refers to Joshua and Zerubbabel; Revelation, to two different men who will be witnesses during the Tribulation.

4. Summary

The night visions have been moving toward a climax. The promise of judgment is given in the second vision; the restoration of Jerusalem, in the third; and the cleansing of the priesthood and the nation, in the fourth. This fifth vision reveals the power for building the temple by Joshua and Zerubbabel. How important for believers today to recognize that God's work is beyond human resources. The Spirit of God is still the source of God's activity and the moving force in the work of God.

C. The Sixth Vision: The Scroll and the Ephah (5:1–11)

Zechariah sees two visions in this chapter: a scroll and an ephah. Some commentators believe that these should be viewed as two separate visions; others argue that there is only one vision with two aspects. This latter view is probably correct since the introductory clause "Then I lifted up my eyes" (5:1) is not repeated in 5:5, where the ephah comes in. However, whether it is one or two visions, the symbols are so closely related that they should be treated as one.

1. The Vision of the Scroll (5:1–2)

Zechariah sees a flying scroll (5:1). A scroll, in biblical times, was made of leather pieces sewn together into a long strip and rolled up for storage. The scroll of Zechariah's vision is a giant piece of leather, unrolled and flying through the air.

The interpreting angel asks Zechariah what he sees, and Zechariah explains the vision (5:2). He gives the dimensions of the leather scroll—it is 20 cubits by 10 cubits or about 30 by 15 feet. (The scroll of Isaiah found at Qumran is about 24 feet long.)

The significance of the dimensions is not given, but it is unlikely that a detail such as this would be added simply to suggest that the scroll was large. These measurements are found for only two other items in the Bible: the porch of Solomon's temple (1 Kings 6:3) and the holy place of the tabernacle (Exod. 26:15–25). The dimensions of the tabernacle are not given explicitly but deduced from the 20 boards, each of which was 1 1/2 cubits wide for a total of 30 cubits. The width was 6 boards (equivalent to 9 cubits), then 2 corner boards whose dimensions are not given. On the assumption that the Holy of Holies was square, it would probably be 10 by 10, leaving 20 by 10 for the holy place, a dimension given by Josephus (Antiquities, 3.6.3). Consequently, it is legitimate to relate the flying scroll to the temple and tabernacle. (The lampstand of chapter 3 came from the tabernacle also.)

The connection of the vision to the tabernacle calls attention to the fact that the tabernacle represents the place where God dwells among His people. The very word used for the tabernacle is from the Hebrew word for *to dwell* and means "the place of God's dwelling." When a holy God dwells among His people, He demands righteous conduct from them. Therefore, this vision indicates God's righteous indignation with sin. He will judge those who violate His holy requirements.

2. The Interpretation of the Scroll (5:3–4)

The interpreting angel says that the scroll represents the curse that is going out over the face of the whole earth (5:3). The reference to the curse that comes upon those who disobey the law of God indicates that the vision pertains to the covenant relation between God and His people. It shows that God's judgment goes out from His holy place upon those who disobey Him. Furthermore, the entire land of Israel is involved in the curse. God's judgment will not overlook anyone who is breaking His law.

There are two sins written on the scroll: stealing and perjury. These are the third and eighth commandments, and thus, the middle commandment in each group of five. They are probably listed because of their central position in the commandments, not because they are the worst among other sins. They serve as samples and summaries. James reminds his hearers that if one keeps "the whole law and yet stumbles in one *point*," he becomes guilty of all the law (James 2:10).

Apparently, there is writing on both sides of the scroll. The NASB has properly translated the Hebrew: "Surely everyone who steals will be purged away according to the writing on one side."

The thief and the perjurer must be punished. The word translated *cut off* (KJV) and *purged away* (NASB) normally means "to be innocent." However, there are three places where the word means "swept away" or "purged away" (Isa. 3:26; Jer. 30:11; 46:28). Thus, those who break the law of God will be judged. The curse of God will go throughout the land of Judah. It will search out the lawbreaker, take up residence, and destroy both the timbers and the stones of that house. Therefore, God will utterly judge that person (5:4).

The meaning of this vision can be determined by comparing it with three of the other visions. The opening message (1:1–6) speaks of God's anger against Israel and warns the Jews of Zechariah's day not to make the same mistake their fathers made. In the horns/craftsmen vision (1:18–21), God indicated that His wrath against Israel was executed by her foes; however, God was angry at the nations for going beyond His judgment in their punishment of Israel. Chapter 3 not only shows the sinfulness of Israel, but also the promise that God will remove the iniquity of that land in one single day (3:9).

Likewise, there is a promise of judgment and deliverance in chapter 5. The sinfulness of the Jews at this time is very evident from the Books of Ezra and Nehemiah. God declares that those Jews who sin against the holy law of God will be punished for that sinfulness. The message of hope, however, is found in the second aspect of the vision (5:5–11).

3. The Vision of the Ephah (5:5–11)

The interpreting angel asks Zechariah to look at a second flying object. The scroll/ephah vision is comparable to that of the horns and craftsmen and makes sense when seen as two aspects of the sin problem. The scroll represents judgment on sin; the ephah represents the removal of sin.

a. The Ephah (5:5–6). Zechariah, looking but not comprehending, asks about the significance of the vision. The ephah was the largest measure in the Old Testament and held between five and ten gallons; however, since the ephah of this vision is large enough to hold a woman (5:7), this basket must be much larger.

The ephah, as well as the scroll, is "going out." This similar action supports the idea that these two symbols are part of one vision.

b. The "Appearance" of the Ephah (5:6). The angel says, "This is their appearance in all the land." The word translated *resemblance* or *appearance* is literally, *their eye.* The use of *eye* for *appearance* is common enough (cf. Lev. 13:55). *Their* would refer to the people in all the land who are lying and perjuring themselves. They "look" like liars and perjurers.

c. The Contents of the Ephah (5:7–8). The interpreting angel has said, "This is the ephah," and, "This is their appearance" (5:6). Now he says, "This is a woman" (5:7). However, before the woman can be seen, a lead cover must be lifted from the ephah. The KJV says "talent of lead;" the NASB, "a lead cover." The Hebrew word in question means basically something round and is used to describe a geographical area (cf. Gen. 13:10, 11). It is later used for a round weight and then a unit of weight or a talent. The NASB is probably correct in using the word in a nontechnical sense as a round lead cover. It is lead because it must hold down the woman who is trying to get out of the ephah.

d. The Meaning of the Woman (5:8). The angel now explains what the woman represents. "This," he says, "is wickedness." Some argue that wickedness in this context is idolatry which was removed from Judaism at this time. They base this on the fact that the word is definite, *"the* wickedness," but so is the curse (5:3) and the ephah (5:6). The Hebrew word for wickedness is used for all kinds of sin, as it is here. Two sins were written on the scroll as *typical* representations of sin, and the wickedness in the ephah also represents sin in general.

The angel then throws the woman down into the ephah, indicating that she was struggling to escape. Then the lead cover, which had been lifted to give Zechariah a peek, is thrown back down on the opening of the ephah.

So far the vision indicates that "wickedness" has been placed in a large container, tied in with two broken commandments of 5:3–4. Furthermore, she is being removed from the land, in spite of her resistance.

e. The Removal of Sin (5:9–11). Zechariah lifts up his eyes and sees two women moving off with wind in their wings so they are traveling swiftly. As if in afterthought, Zechariah says that the woman had wings like those of a stork, an unclean bird, probably chosen here because of its large, strong wings. These two women with their storklike wings lift up the basket and fly off into the sky (5:9, lit., between earth and heaven).

Zechariah then asks the interpreting angel to tell him where the women are taking the ephah (5:10). The answer is that they have gone to build a house for her in the land of Shinar, and when it is ready, she will be set there on her pedestal. The feminine pronoun "her" can refer to the ephah (feminine in Hebrew) or to the woman called "wickedness." In this context it must refer to the woman. The word *house* is common in Hebrew for *temple*, whether the temple of the one true God (1 Kings 7:12), of Baal (2 Kings 10:23), or of Ashtoreth (1 Sam. 31:10). So the house in 5:11 is a shrine with the idol "wickedness" set up on a pedestal within it.

The place to which "wickedness" is being removed is the land of Shinar. This is the ancient name for southern Mesopotamia (Gen. 10:10). Outside of the early occurrences, it only appears in Isaiah 11:11, Daniel 1:2, and here. It was in the land of Shinar that Nimrod, whose very name means rebellion, built his cities (Gen. 10:10). It was also in Shinar that the people built the tower of Babel in rebellion against God (Gen. 11:1–9).

In the vision of chapter 5, sin is being removed from the land of Israel as promised in 3:9 and is being taken to another place, namely, the land of Shinar. This means that God is removing sin from Israel and setting it up among those who reject Him and adopt an anti-God system as the builders of Babel did long ago.

Revelation 17–18 speaks of "mystery Babylon," that embodiment of all evil that God will judge. This concentration of evil in the place of its origin will take place in the last days before the Battle of Armageddon and the establishment of the millennial kingdom. Thus, God will remove evil from the people of Israel as He prepares them to be His people. He will also judge those nations who will become even more wicked in the last days.

4. Conclusion

The meaning of the vision is for the future: God will remove sin from Israel. For Zechariah's day, however, it also means that violation of God's law would be judged. Jews living in the sixth century before Christ need to understand the seriousness of sin. The vision, to that extent, applies to them, but its fulfillment will take place with the return of Christ.

God's people of any dispensation must always be aware of the seriousness of sin. God will deal with it in His own children, as well as in unbelievers. He expects those who know Him to live holy lives, even as they anticipate that day when all will be set right in His holy kingdom.

Paul teaches that the law brings a curse, since no one is able to keep it (Gal. 3:10). The law itself is good because it reflects the holiness of God, but man's inability to obey it brings him under its judgment. Yet, Christ bore the curse by becoming accursed Himself (Gal. 3:13). How blessed is God's redemption!

For Further Study

1. Use a concordance to look up the word "Satan" in the Old Testament. Explain his purpose in the vision of chapter 3.

2. Read Exodus 28 for a description of the priests' clothing. Look for a picture of a priest in a Bible dictionary.

3. In light of the recent return from the exile, what is the message of the cleansing of Joshua? What are the implications of that message for God's servants today?

4. Draw a picture of the lampstand in chapter 4 as you perceive it.

5. The statement in 4:6 is often quoted. What does it mean in its context and how can it be applied today?

6. Locate the Ten Commandments in Exodus 20 and identify the sins mentioned in chapter 5.

Chapter 4

Vision of Judgment
(Zechariah 6:1–8)

The series of night visions comes to a conclusion much as it began. The first vision shows God's representatives giving a report of their travels throughout the earth (1:7–17). The final vision also has horses but they are different from those in chapter 1 because they are harnessed to chariots. Chariots were not used for transportation, but for war. Consequently, this vision deals with God's judgment.

A. The Symbols (6:1–3)

There are four chariots "going out" just as the scroll and the women were "going out" (6:1, 5). A task is to be performed. These chariots go out from between two mountains that are made of bronze. The chariots are pulled by horses (probably two to a chariot) that are different colors.

The first team is red; the second team, black; the third team, white. The only difficult description is given to the fourth group of horses. The NASB has "strong and dappled;" the KJV, "grisled and bay." The Hebrew word translated *dappled* (NASB) or *grisled* (KJV) is more difficult, especially because of 6:7. Normally this Hebrew word means "strong." Because a color would fit the context better, some interpreters have tried to spell the Hebrew word differently to denote a color (KJV), but its normal meaning should be used. The issue of the colors will be discussed again later.

The horses come from between two mountains made of bronze. (The Hebrew word is translated by the KJV throughout

the Bible as *brass,* but it is now known that the material was an
alloy of copper and tin that produces bronze.) Bronze was a hard
material and was used in the tabernacle, especially for the large
altar of sacrifice. Usually the mountains are assumed to represent judgment, since the chariots going out from them are for
judgment. Joel 3 (especially vv. 2, 12) points to a time when God
will bring all nations to the Valley of Jehoshaphat. The name
Jehoshaphat means "Jehovah will judge." From early times, this
valley has been identified with the Kidron Valley east of
Jerusalem. If this identity is correct, the mountains on either
side of it, Zion and Olivet, *could* refer to the two mountains in
Zechariah 6. Zechariah 14:4 indicates that Jehovah is coming to
the Mount of Olives for judgment. Therefore, the symbolism
may indicate that God is going to judge the nations from
between these two mountains, that is, in the Valley of Jehoshaphat or Kidron.

B. The Interpretation of the Vision (6:4–8)

Zechariah asks what the symbols mean (6:4). The interpreting angel begins to explain in 6:5.

1. The Four Winds (6:5–8)

The angel states that the four chariots are the four winds of
heaven going out from standing before the Lord of all the earth.
The angel is switching the imagery from chariots to winds. He
has already referred to the four winds of heaven in 1:10. The
four winds probably refer to the four points of the earth,
meaning that Israel has been scattered all over the earth. The
Hebrew word for *wind* can also mean "spirit." As a result, some
argue that the Holy Spirit is the intent of the symbol; others
believe that the winds signify the swiftness of God's judgment.

God is at work. He deals with the whole world and will
bring swift and final judgment upon it. In addition, this vision
indicates the universality of God's control. He is in charge of the
whole earth (cf. 6:5, the Lord of all the earth).

There are three major problems in the vision of the four
chariots: (1) the significance, if any, of the number four; (2) the
significance, if any, of the colors, and (3) the omission of the red

horses in the explanation (6:5–8) where the spotted and strong horses are separated.

2. The Number Four

The text does not explain the number four, and that omission should bring caution to any effort to attribute meaning to it. It is tempting to see the four kingdoms of Daniel 2 and 7 (Babylon, Medo-Persia, Greece, and Rome). Certainly, Zechariah would have been familiar with Daniel's writings. The four horns of Zechariah 1 are explicitly identified with the nations "raising up a horn against Judah." However, these chariots (chapter 6) are not said to represent nations, and they seem to be carrying out God's judgment against others. The number four probably represents God's control of the four quarters of the earth and His intention to judge all the earth.

3. The Colors

The three passages in the Bible with different colored horses are as follows:

Zechariah 1	Zechariah 6	Revelation 6
Red	Red	White—conquering
Sorrel	Black	Red—war
White	White	Black—famine
	Dappled/strong	Pale—death, hell

Each of the differently colored horses in the Book of Revelation is identified with a concept: the white horse refers to conquering; the red, war; the black, famine; the pale horse, death and hades. Since three of those same four colors appear in Zechariah 6, it is tempting to apply the same meanings to the colors. However, the differences between Zechariah and Revelation and the fact that the text does not provide any interpretation of the colors argue against interpreting the colors in Zechariah 6. It may be that the only purpose of the colors is to distinguish the horses in the interpretation that follows.

4. The Absence of the Red Horses

The first statement of the vision says that the horses are red, black, white, and strong and dappled, but the interpretation of the vision says that the horses are black, white, dappled, and strong. If the colors have no inherent significance, the problem of the missing red horses can be explained more easily. Those who see the four chariots as four kingdoms are hard-pressed to explain the new division of the interpretation. If the vision is only showing that God controls the four quarters of the earth, all that is needed is a group of four in both the symbol (red, black, white, and strong/dappled) and its interpretation (black, white, dappled, and strong).

5. The Task of the Chariots

The angel says that the four winds/chariots are "going forth after standing before the LORD in all the earth." The word *standing* appears also in Job 1:6 and 2:1 where it refers to Satan and the "sons of God." In Job, the angelic hosts as servants of God "present" themselves before God for orders. Even Satan presents himself. In this vision, the chariots have been in the presence of God to receive orders. The phrase, "LORD of all the earth" (used in Josh. 3:11; Ps. 97:5; Micah 4:13; Zech. 4:14; 6:5) indicates that God is the sovereign Master of the universe. This message is to encourage Israel by teaching them that God is in charge of this world system no matter how twisted and perverse the people and events that make it up. Through His agents, He is keeping an eye on all that happens.

The angel now speaks of the geographical directions where the chariots are going. The first one (black horse) is going forth to the land of the north. The greatest danger to Israel always lay in the north. Assyria, Babylonia, and (in Zechariah's day) Medo-Persia all came from the east, but they had to come up around the fertile crescent and go south to Israel. Hence, they always came from the north. Zechariah was told in chapter 1 that God would eventually deal with those nations that had afflicted Israel. The same promise is conveyed by this chariot. The nations of the north, be they Assyria, Babylonia, Medo-Persia or whoever, will be judged by God. He is fully aware of the problems of injustice and inequity and will deal with them.

The second chariot with white horses goes out after the first. No doubt, this chariot is to reinforce the first one. The strongest opposition to Israel comes from the north, and thus the strongest means is needed to judge those nations. Hence, two chariots go in that direction.

The third chariot with spotted horses goes to the south. The south normally refers to Egypt. Their repression of Israel during the latter's sojourn there is well known. Less well known are the attacks against Israel carried on after Solomon's time and up to the fall of the kingdom under Zedekiah. God will judge Egypt for her part in persecuting Israel.

The fourth chariot, drawn by the strong horses, goes out looking for a place to patrol and to carry out God's orders. Since the two main centers of resistance have been taken care of, this chariot does not know where to go. Someone tells it (the Lord of all the earth?) to go and patrol the earth. Therefore, God is "covering all the bases," not just the north and the south, but the whole world. The Jews of Zechariah's day have nothing to fear; God is in charge and He will effect His divine will.

So far the task of the chariots has not been explained, but in 6:8 the interpreting angel tells Zechariah the purpose of the vision. "Those who are going to the land of the north have appeased my wrath in the land of the north" indicates that the primary direction of the vision is toward the north countries. The Hebrew word translated *appeased* (NASB) and *quieted* (KJV) has a basic meaning of "rest," then "to give rest." The meaning here is the same as Ezekiel 5:13; 16:42; and 21:17. When God puts His anger to rest, He has satisfied it or appeased it. The meaning of 6:8 is that God's spirit of anger against the nations will be put to rest (appeased) when He brings judgment against them.

For Further Study

1. Read 1:7–17 again and compare it with the vision of this chapter.

2. Do you see any implications from this vision for God's activities in the world today?

Chapter 5

Conclusion and Summary to the Seven Visions

The night visions of Zechariah have a pattern. They begin with horses and end with horses and chariots (see J. G. Baldwin, *Haggai, Zechariah, Malachi,* for an excellent discussion on the structure of the first six chapters). It remains now to examine the total message of the visions and to attempt to determine the time of their fulfillment.

The people of Zechariah's day needed a challenge to complete the temple; they needed conviction of their sins; and they needed encouragement for the future. All of these things are accomplished through the visions.

The first vision (the horsemen) teaches that God is sovereign and therefore in charge of the events of history. He has been angry at Israel for "these seventy years," but He will have mercy on her. Furthermore, the temple will be built within the city. This vision is to encourage God's people in the midst of unpromising circumstances.

The second vision (horns/craftsmen) teaches that God is going to judge the nations who have persecuted Israel. While many of those nations have fallen, Israel still suffers persecution. The vision of the horns/craftsmen is for the future when God will have judged all those nations who mistreated God's people.

The language of the third vision (the measuring line) is so extensive and intensive that it can only apply to the future. Israel is to take courage in the fact that some day God will build Jerusalem, dwell in her midst, and bring many nations to her for redemption. That has not taken place. The fact that the promise is deferred makes it no less encouraging. Each generation could pray and hope that it would happen to them, but it has not yet happened. It will take place in the Millennium when Christ establishes His kingdom on earth.

The fourth vision (Joshua) teaches first of all that God is restoring the priesthood after the captivity. But it also teaches that God is going to cleanse Israel from her sin. The language of the vision indicates that the ultimate fulfillment of this vision pertains to the end times when God will remove the iniquity of the land in "one day" and will bring forth his servant the "Branch," the Messiah.

The fifth vision (the lampstand) teaches that God will use Zerubbabel to build the temple. This was an urgent problem in that day, and God promised to deal with it. Part of the reason for raising up Zechariah and Haggai is to urge the completion of the temple. This vision is, therefore, one of hope and encouragement in connection with the temple.

The sixth vision (the scroll and the ephah) shows that God was judging sin in Zechariah's day. The law was being violated and therefore had to be dealt with. At the same time, the removal of iniquity to "Shinar" should be related to God's promise to remove the iniquity of that land in one day. Israel will not be cleansed of her sins until the Messiah returns.

The final vision (chariots) brings us full circle. The first vision of the horsemen shows God's sovereign control; the last vision of chariots shows that God is going to judge the nations and vindicate His holiness.

These visions are therefore a sort of encapsulated theology of God's dealings with the post-exilic community of His people. He will restore them; the temple will be rebuilt through His enablement; the Messiah will one day come and Israel will be cleansed from her sin. God will dwell in the midst of Jerusalem, and all nations will come to Him for redemption.

For Further Study

1. Summarize the seven visions.
2. What overall message do the visions present?

Chapter 6

Special Messages to the Returnees
(Zechariah 6:9–8:23)

A. Message to the Babylonian Jews: "The Crowning of Joshua" (6:9–15)

Almost two decades had passed since the first group of Jews struggled back to the desolate city of Jerusalem to reconstitute the Jewish community under the leadership of Zerubbabel. The Jews who remained in Babylon had established their own community, but there was an obvious tie to the holy city of Jerusalem and the temple whose construction was now resuming and about which Zechariah had just received visions promising its completion.

This same situation prevailed in New Testament times when Jews came to Jerusalem from all over the world to renew their spiritual heritage (cf. Acts 21). They were called the *diaspora* in Greek, "the sown ones," that is, sown in the world as seed in a field. The Hebrew word is *golah,* the exiled ones. Representatives from the *golah* came to Jerusalem, probably on a pilgrimage, possibly to offer financial assistance to the Jews who were struggling for survival in Israel.

This section of the book is not in vision form, and Zechariah returns to the typical prophetic introduction, "The word of the LORD came to me." Previously, the messages from God came to Zechariah in vision form, but now God's message is presented directly to the people by symbolic action. God instructs Zechariah to take silver and gold from certain people who came from

Babylon and to make crowns and place them on the head of Joshua the high priest.

1. The Personages (6:10)

The names of the visitors are Heldai, Tobijah, and Jedaiah. No emphasis should be put on the names except to note that they are Hebrew, not pagan names. The Hebrew word translated *take* is a form used for emphasis to stress the importance of this act. God then tells Zechariah to come to the house of Josiah son of Zephaniah to meet these three men from Babylon. Josiah (probably named after the last good king of Judah) has shown proper hospitality in receiving these men from Babylon into his home. By so doing, he will receive the blessing accorded to them.

This symbolic event (the crowning of Joshua) probably took place the day after the final "vision of the night." Joshua was the center of the fourth vision (chap. 3), and he is the center of the symbolic action in this chapter. Because of the messianic implications of this section, critics want to substitute, or at least add, Zerubbabel's name, but there is absolutely no warrant for it. This act of crowning points to the future Messiah. It is carried out in Zechariah's day to encourage the Jews to recognize that God's hand is in all of history.

2. The Symbolic Action (6:11)

The Lord tells Zechariah to receive gold and silver from the three men. This offering shows that the Jewish community in Babylon, though they had been unwilling to join in the returning Jews under Zerubbabel, still wanted a part in building the temple and reestablishing Judaism in the holy city. Much the same situation prevails today. Few American Jews have been willing to go to Israel to identify with her in her suffering, but they have been anxious to help financially. In spite of that incongruity, Zechariah is told to receive the offering and to make "an *ornate* crown" (KJV, *crowns*). The reason for the difference in translations is that the Hebrew word for crown is plural. Commentators disagree on the significance of the plural. The word *crown* appears in the Hebrew Bible twenty-three times. Outside these two occurrences, it is plural only in Job

31:36. The Hebrew often uses a plural to denote complexity or immensity, but even in Esther 8:15 where the crown is said to be large, the singular is used. It is probable, therefore, that the plural form here has more significance than mere "ornateness." Two crowns are in view—one silver, one gold—and they are probably intertwined to make it easier to put them on Joshua's head.

It is important to note that no high priest in the Old Testament was ever crowned king. The high priest wore a turban (cf. 3:5), but not a crown. The offices of priest and king were certainly kept apart. Uzziah was punished by God with leprosy for usurping the priestly role (2 Chron. 26:16–21). It was not until the Maccabean Period (second century B.C.) that the priestly family of Mattathias assumed the kingly rule. Since Joshua could not possibly hold both offices, he is the prefigurement of another who will receive the crown and fill both offices of king and priest. That person is the Messiah.

3. The Message of the Symbolism (6:12–13)

Zechariah is commanded to speak the words that come from Jehovah of hosts. This title for God speaks of His omnipotence. The Lord commands Zechariah to say, "Behold, a man whose name is Branch." Joshua the high priest is a type of the coming one whose name is Branch. The background for this title is given in the discussion of chapter 3. The early Jewish paraphrase (Targum) of this verse says, "Behold the man, Messiah is his name." Thus from ancient times, this passage has been interpreted to refer to the coming Messiah: He is to branch out from where He is. The insignificant beginning of the Messiah is the theme of Isaiah 11:1 and Isaiah 53:2, and Zechariah is told that the Messiah will sprout up (as a branch) from where He is, that is, His lowly beginnings. Furthermore, He will build the temple.

Some argue that this building is Zerubbabel's temple, since he was told not only that he would lay the foundation of the temple, but that he would also set on the cap stone (4:9). It is for this reason that critical scholars want to see Zerubbabel's name here rather than Joshua's, and are even willing to change the text. However, the reference to the coming Branch, who will both rule and act as priest, points to the temple of the future. The relevance for Joshua and Zechariah's time comes from the encouragement the promise gives. As the vision of the lamp-stand (chapter 4) was designed to encourage Zerubbabel and the people to complete the task of building the sixth-century temple, this chapter shows Israel a greater work of God extending far beyond anything Israel of that day knew. Ezekiel speaks of a temple during the Millennium (Ezek. 40–48), and the crowning of Joshua is a symbolic prediction of the millennial temple, which the Branch, the Messiah, will build.

Further description of this coming one is given in 6:13. Not only will He build the temple (this phrase is repeated, and additional ministries for the Branch are added), He will also bear the regal glory of kingship and sit and rule upon His throne. No human priest is permitted to sit while ministering, since his work is never finished (Heb. 10:11–12). Thus, Joshua can only be a prefigurement of the One who will be both king and priest. This Messiah is the One to whom Jehovah said, "Sit at my right hand" and "rule in the midst of thy enemies" (Ps. 110:1, 2). It was also said of Him in the same psalm, "Thou art a priest forever after the order of Melchizedek" (Ps. 110:4). The Lord Jesus Christ is still coming to sit upon the throne of His father David (Luke 1:32). He has already acted the part of priest when He died on the cross to redeem sinners (1 Peter 2:24) and He is now interceding for believers (Rom. 8:34), but His kingly rule is yet to come.

The final part of the coming Branch's ministry is in some ways the most intriguing. "The counsel of peace will be between the two offices" (6:13). The word *counsel* describes wise action that results in peace (cf. Isa. 11:2). This peace has to do with reconciliation (peace with God) as well as inner peace. Isa. 53:5 has the same Hebrew construction and means "the chastisement that *produced* our peace." Some think *both* refers to the Father and the Son, but it is more likely referring to the two offices of "ruler" and "priest." Christ acts in both capacities, and between these two offices will be the counsel leading to peace in the world.

4. The Crowns as a Memorial (6:14–15)

The crowns are to be deposited in the temple as a memorial to these men who brought the gifts to Jerusalem and as a reminder to all who see them that God will carry out His purposes.

There are two differences between the names in 6:14 and 6:10. First, Heldai is referred to as Helem. Some conclude that a mistake has occurred when the text was copied through the centuries, but it may be simply a different name for the same man. Second, Hen appears for Josiah. Keil is probably correct in assuming that Hen is not a proper name.[1] It is the normal Hebrew word for *grace* or *favor*. The translation would then read, "and for the favor of the son of Zephaniah." Therefore, Josiah had shown gracious hospitality to these fellow Jews from Babylon, and God is taking note of that fact as the crowns are placed in the temple.

5. The Future Participants in God's Work (6:15)

Just as these Jews have come from a distant Babylon, so when God's final work is done in the future, people from distant lands will be involved in it. Then the Jews will truly recognize that God has sent the Angel of Jehovah with these messages to Zechariah and to Israel.

6. The Condition (6:15)

Deuteronomy 28:1 indicates that the enjoyment of the blessing of God is conditioned upon obedience. These promises given to Israel will come to pass if they obey the voice of Jehovah their God.

7. Summary

This first message, given after the visions and in response to the delegation from Babylon, reaches into the future. The present circumstances (the rebuilding of the temple) are the backdrop for the message, but it is a prediction of the coming Messiah who is called the Branch. He will act both as priest and

---

*Keil, The Twelve Minor Prophets, vol. 2 in Biblical Commentary on the Old Testament, pp. 300–01.

king. Zechariah's message is to challenge and encourage the Jews of his day, but his prophetic statements are not limited to that time. The believers are also encouraged with God's future work when He establishes His kingdom on the earth. Therefore, these marvelous promises of the Branch who will build a temple are important to the messianic hope of the Jews.

B. Instruction on True Religion: "The Fast Question" (7:1–14)

Chapter 7 takes place two years after the visions. As in 6:9–15, the form is one of instruction from the Lord, and both of these passages begin with "the word of the LORD came."

By the fourth year of Darius (518 B.C.), the empire was under control and had been extended into India. The Jewish position in Palestine was much more firmly established. Opposition to the building of the temple had been officially squashed (Ezra 6:1–15; Hag. 1:14–15), and now within two years (516 B.C.) the temple would be completed (Ezra 6:15). Many Jews had built fine homes and reestablished the agriculture cycles (Hag. 1:4–6). In light of this improvement, it would be only natural to ask whether the fasts, instituted to commemorate the destruction of the city and temple, should be continued. God's Word to Zechariah is an answer to the question raised by the delegation from Bethel.

1. The Occasion (7:1–2)

The occasion for the prophetic statement in this chapter arose when a delegation came to Jerusalem to entreat the Lord. The time of the message is given in 7:1: "Then it came about in the fourth year of King Darius, that the word of the LORD came to Zechariah on the fourth day of the ninth month, which is Chislev." This verse should be compared with 1:1 and 1:7 and translated as follows: "And so in the fourth year of Darius the king, the word of the LORD came to Zechariah in the fourth day of the ninth month (in Chislev) when Bethel sent . . ."

The KJV says, "When they had sent unto the house of God Sharezer . . ."; NASB, "Now the *town* of Bethel had sent . . ." The word *Bethel* means literally "house of God," as the KJV has translated it. The problem with that translation is that *Bethel* is never used for the temple of Jehovah; therefore, Bethel in this context must be the town lying a few miles north of Jerusalem. It was a border town between Benjamin (Josh. 18:13) and Ephraim (Josh. 16:2). When the northern tribes broke off from Judah, Bethel became a cult center under Jeroboam (1 Kings 12:32–33) because of its ancient connections with the patriarchs (Gen. 12:8; 28:19; 35:1). The city of Bethel learned her lesson through God's chastening. Two hundred and twenty-three men of Bethel had returned from the Exile and apparently rebuilt the city (Ezra 2:28; Neh. 7:32; 11:31). These "men of Bethel" are the subject of the sentence. They now give their allegiance to the priests and prophets of Jerusalem and no longer are involved in the precaptivity paganism of Bethel.

Two of the delegates are named. The first is Sharezer. Sharezer is the pagan name of Sennacherib's son, who, with his brother, killed his father as he was worshiping. Regem-Melech may be a Hebrew name since Regem appears in 1 Chronicles 2:47. In any event these two delegates, along with some of their men, are sent by the city of Bethel to seek God's favor and to ask a question about ritual. The Hebrew idiom "to seek favor" is literally "to soften the face." They were there to petition God to have a soft, tender face toward them.

2. The Question (7:3)

Sharezer and Regemmelech address their question to the priests who were serving in the house of Jehovah of hosts and to the prophets (the house of Jehovah refers to the uncompleted temple). This situation indicates that the prophets and priests are regarded as having equal authority to represent God. The question is, "Shall I weep in the fifth month and abstain, as I have done these many years?"

Fasting had come to be a special form of intercession (2 Sam. 12:16; Ezra 8:21; Esth. 4:3; etc.). The fasting on the fifth month was a memorial to the destruction of the temple by Nebuchadnezzar in 586 B.C. (2 Kings 25:8). Now that the temple is well on the way to restoration and prosperity seems to be more and more possible, the question naturally arises as to the appropriateness of a fast for the temple. The word *abstain* is derived from the same Hebrew word as *Nazirite*. The Nazirite separated himself and devoted himself to God. These people have separated themselves to pray for the temple.

3. The Prophetic Response (7:4–7)

The question is answered negatively in chapter 7 but positively in chapter 8. Zechariah's response goes to the heart of Old Testament religion. The ritual, designed to point to God, too often became an end in itself, and the reality of worship was lost. The word of Jehovah of Hosts that came to Zechariah may seem harsh, particularly to people who appear to be asking a sincere question, but false religion, however sincere, is eternally devastating. God must cut to the heart of the matter and lay open the emptiness of professing religion. Many people are sincere in their beliefs, but if they have not put their personal faith in Christ as Savior, they are eternally lost.

Zechariah is told to speak to all the people of the land and to the priests. This statement lends credence to the argument that the people asking the question are from Bethel. The answer is not sent to Babylon, but it is for the Jews of Palestine and for the priests too. Their ministry is primarily, but not exclusively, one of ritual, so the prophetic word must come from the prophet.

The question God asks them is, "When you fasted and mourned in the fifth and seventh months these seventy years, was it actually for me that you fasted?" (7:5). (The fourth and tenth months are mentioned in 8:19.) The four dates probably refer to the following events. The city was captured by Nebuchadnezzar in the fourth month of 586 B.C. (2 Kings 25:8), and the temple was destroyed in the fifth month (2 Kings 25:8, 9). Governor Gedaliah was murdered in the seventh month (2 Kings 25:25), and the siege of the city had begun in the tenth month (2 Kings 25:1).

God questions the motives of the Jews in 7:5. Was that fast really for the Lord? Did it indicate a repentant heart as they recognized that the city and temple were destroyed because of the overt wickedness of the people? Judah's sin had been denounced strongly and unequivocally by Jeremiah (cf. Jer. 7). The people of his day were taking refuge in the ritual of the temple with the expectation that God could not possibly destroy His own temple. Jeremiah uncovered the hypocrisy of that mentality with surgical precision. Now God asks the returned exiles whether their attitude is any different. Are they not, like their predecessors, hiding under the facade of religious ritual that really has nothing to do with God?

"These seventy years" refers to a period predicted by Jeremiah in 25:1–14. That period began with the destruction of the temple in 586 B.C. and was concluded with the completion of the temple in 516 B.C. For this entire period, the Jews have been bewailing the loss of the temple, much like the Jews of a later generation who went to the western retaining wall to bewail the destruction of Herod's temple in A.D. 70. The seventy years are almost completed. Should they stop what they have been doing? The answer is shocking, "What you have been doing was meaningless anyway; what difference does it make whether it is stopped?"

God presses His indictment further in 7:6. Not only was their religious practice a farce, since it was only for the benefit of the practitioner and had nothing to do with God, but even the normal practices of life (eating and drinking) were for selfish motives.

God, as a jealous God, demands all from His children. These people had learned to compartmentalize their thinking so that part of their lives were devoted to religious ritual and part to normal living. This practice always leads to spiritual lethargy. Only when the entire life is given to God does one realize true spirituality.

Furthermore, God reminds them that this same message was presented through the former prophets who had also preached that obedience to God's Word was to take precedence over ritual (7:7). That message was delivered in a time when Jerusalem and its environs were in a state of health, and yet God threatened them with destruction. The analogy is clear. The Jews are beginning to achieve a measure of success in the rebuilding of the temple and the reconstruction of their community. At the same time they, like their forefathers, must learn to have a genuine relation to Jehovah and obey His words.

4. The Repetition of History (7:8–14)

The content of God's message to the pre-exilic people is given in these verses. The normal translation of 7:9 would be "Thus says the LORD of hosts," but the context demands a past tense, "thus *did* the LORD of hosts say," that is, in the period before the Exile.

a. The Message of the Former Prophets (7:8–10). The earlier prophets preached that true faith issues in social justice (7:9–10). The nation of Israel was a theocratic kingdom and as such was required to treat the members of the kingdom with equity and justice. They were to carry out true judgment. When people had a complaint, it was to be dealt with honestly. Furthermore, they were to practice kindness and mercy toward one another. The word *kindness* is a word that has to do with the faithfulness of God and those in His covenant. The people who receive that kindness are called saints. Now the Israelites themselves are called upon to show that same kindness. The word *compassion* is plural in the Hebrew and thus connotes individual acts of compassion making up the whole.

The vulnerable members of the believers' society are dealt with next (7:10). The widow, the orphans and the foreigner are especially open to oppression. With no one to be their advocate, they are at the mercy of their stronger neighbors. True faith, said the former prophets, would result in these people not being oppressed.

Finally, they are instructed not to devise evil in their hearts against a brother. The word *devise* is a serious word. It involves premeditation. Members of the theocratic community were not to plan any kind of evil against their fellow members.

b. The Response of the Forefathers (7:11–12). The pre-exilic Jews rejected the message of the prophets: "They refused to pay attention" (7:11). This was not a sin of ignorance but of arrogance. Their disobedience was blatant (the Book of Jeremiah portrays this crass rejection of God in graphic terms; cf. especially Jer. 44:15–19). God says secondly that they turned a stubborn shoulder. This metaphor is that of an ox that whirls to the side to avoid having the yoke placed on his neck. In the same manner Israel has refused God's instruction. Thirdly, they stopped their ears (lit., "made their ears heavy") so they would not hear. It is no wonder that God told Isaiah to make Israel's ears heavy as an act of judgment (Isa. 6:10). Finally, they made their hearts as hard as flint so as not to hear the Law and the words Jehovah had sent them.

God, speaking through Zechariah, has piled accusation upon accusation against the forebears of the present generation. To show the extent of their sinful attitude, He reminds them that this message came through His Spirit as well as through the prophets. Israel stood condemned without excuse. As a result, "great wrath came from the LORD of hosts." It is small wonder that the patience of God was finally exhausted. The long promised judgment of God came with devastating force against the covenant people who thought they could do as they pleased because they were under the covenant. What a miscalculation of the righteousness and judgment of God!

One of the great theological problems with which the returning Jewish community had to grapple was the judgment of God upon His chosen people. Why should Israel be in such devastation when surrounding pagan nations seemed to be enjoying His favor. The answer is that "from everyone who has been given much shall much be required" (Luke 12:48). Israel's favored position brought great responsibility as well as privilege. The Exile was their punishment for abusing their position to further their own ends rather than to glorify God.

c. The Warning to the People of Zechariah's Day (7:13–14). The time of the Hebrew verbs must be followed closely to determine the intent of this passage. Zechariah, to describe the problem of the pre-exilic Jews, says, "And it came to pass as he called and they would not listen . . ." Then he cites the words of the former prophets: "Thus, 'I will sweep them away . . .'" This is a summary of the message of the former prophets. Jeremiah 23:19–20 has similar language, including the whirlwind metaphor. Deuteronomy 28:64 speaks of scattering them among all people where they will serve gods, which their fathers had not known. At this point Israel and Judah had only been scattered among the cities of the kingdom of Assyria and Babylonia. The prophecy had its beginning in 722 B.C. with the deportation of

Israel and 586 B.C. with the deportation of Judah, but its ultimate fulfillment extends throughout all time.

The result of the disobedience by the forefathers is found in 7:14: "Thus the land is desolated behind them, so that no one went back and forth, for they made the pleasant land desolate."

5. Summary

This section is reminiscent of 1:3–6. Because Israel would not learn the lessons of history, she was doomed to repeat them. Zechariah is trying to turn Israel from the worn path of iniquity, trodden by their fathers who were judged for their sin.

C. Instruction on the Future of Zion: "The Fast Question, Continued" (8:1–23)

The seventh chapter addressed the issue of whether the fasts commemorating the loss of the temple should be continued. God's response was to chide them for the hypocrisy of their action. The ritual of keeping fasts had no impact on the reality of living. The mention of the fasts in 8:19 indicates that the same issue is being pursued in chapter eight.

The message in chapter eight, however, is an encouraging one. This chapter is replete with promises, some of which are among the most marvelous in the Old Testament. As if to assure the reader of the integrity of the promises, Zechariah speaks in the name of Jehovah of hosts. This title for God appears fifty-four times in Zechariah, and eighteen of those are in chapter 8. As the name El Shaddai (Almighty God) is used during the patriarchal period, but not later, so Jehovah of hosts is used in Israel's later history but not in the Pentateuch. It is a favorite title for God in the prophets, especially Isaiah, Jeremiah, and Zechariah. The stress is on God's omnipotence as the head of the armies of heaven fighting on behalf of God's people.

This chapter may be divided into two major sections. The first is 8:1–18 ("and the word of the LORD of hosts came"); the second, 8:19–23 ("and the word of the LORD of hosts came to me"). There are ten "oracles" or "sayings" introduced by the phrase "thus says the LORD of hosts" (vv. 2, 3, 4, 6, 7, 9, 14, 19, 20, and 23). Verse 3 is included even though it has only "Thus says the LORD" because it seems to be the same introductory clause.

1. First Segment: Encouragement to the Returnees (8:1–19)

There is a close parallel between chapter 8 and chapters 1 and 2, as the following table illustrates.

Chapter Eight	Chapters One and Two
I am zealous for Zion (v. 2).	I am zealous for Jerusalem and for Zion (1:14).
I will return to Zion and dwell in the midst of Jerusalem (v. 3).	Behold I am coming and I will dwell in your midst (2:10).
Old men and women will yet live in the streets of Jerusalem (vv. 4–5).	My cities will be spread out from so much goodness (1:17).
Behold, I am going to deliver people from the east land and west land (v. 7).	Woe, woe, flee from the north land (2:6).
And many people and numerous nations shall come to seek Jehovah of hosts in Jerusalem (v. 22).	And many nations shall be joined to Jehovah in that day, and they shall be my people (2:11).

The vision in chapter 2 is of the Millennium. The Jews of Zechariah's day were encouraged to know that God would ultimately establish His kingdom on earth. Chapter 8, too, is a strongly encouraging word following on the heels of God's rebuke in chapter 7. Now, in the manner of a good father, He encourages them with comforting promises. Sometimes the promises clearly extend to the end times, but at other times they seem to be contemporary with Zechariah. Therefore, the question to be resolved in 8:1–19 is whether the promises are applied to Israel in Zechariah's time or in the eschatological future.

God has indeed brought Israel back. The temple is in the

process of being built, and the mountain of Zion can again be called "the holy mountain" (8:3). God is obviously dwelling in the midst of Israel in spite of her sins (8:3). There is a measure of prosperity for Israel (8:4). At the same time, none of this language was fulfilled completely in Zechariah's time. It must be concluded that the final fulfillment of 8:1–19 is yet to come during the Millennium.

God's revelation of the future, however, often has an anchor in the present. Matthew 10 is a classic example. Christ sends out the disciples to proclaim that the kingdom of heaven is at hand. He explains to them the nature of their ministry and the response of people to it. But suddenly, without warning or transition, he jumps to the future time (10:16–26) and even says that they will not have gone through all the cities of Israel before the Son of Man returns!

It is important to understand, then, that while some Old Testament prophecies have application to contemporary times, many of them find their ultimate fulfillment in the future. Any Jew of that day would know that the scenes depicted by Zechariah (8:3–4) were not yet in effect (cf. Ezra-Nehemiah for the actual conditions). But they could take heart in the fact that the work begun by God in their day would come to glorious fruition in "the latter days."

a. **Oracle #1: God's Attitude (8:2).** God is jealous for Zion. The verb "jealous" is in the perfect tense, indicating a state of mind. The idea of jealousy, when applied to God, must be divorced from the human perspective. In people, jealousy is usually a negative, destructive force, but in a perfect God, jealousy is His righteous concern for the purity of His people (cf. 2 Cor. 11:2). In 1:13–15, the angel laments that Israel is languishing while the nations are prospering. God's response is similar here. He is jealous with a great jealousy. He tells Israel that He is a jealous God (Exod. 20:5) whose very name is Jealous (Exod. 34:14). Jehovah God in His tender mercy has shown great concern for His chosen people.

b. **Oracles #2–3: God's Activity (8:3–4).** The vision of the man with the measuring line (2:1–13) is a promise of God's millennial blessing upon the city of Jerusalem. The prosperous city is said to be spread out without walls because of the large number of people and animals living in her. In chapter 8, the picture is also a tranquil one. Old men and women will sit along the streets of Jerusalem. The old man with a staff in his hand will be there, and the joyous laughter of children will ring in the streets. This delightful picture shows the two most vulnerable kinds of people living securely. In that great future Millennium, God will provide all the people a secure and happy place to dwell.

c. **Oracle #4: The Amazement of the People (8:6).** As the small remnant of the Jews view their situation, they probably wonder if Zechariah's prophecy could ever be fulfilled. So in the future (in those days), the Jewish remnant will shake their heads in disbelief. The word translated *difficult* refers to something miraculous (cf. Gen. 18:14). No matter how impossible something may seem to be to God's people, God does not view it in the same way. This restoration of Israel to a place of blessing and prosperity is not at all hard for God—He will do it!

d. **Oracle #5: The Return of Israel (8:7–8).** The content of 8:7 argues further that the time of the fulfillment of this prophecy must be in the last days. In Zechariah's day, Israel was exiled to the east (or north as in 2:6). But this promise is that the regathering of Israel will also be from the west. It was only in later history that Jews began to live in Asia Minor, Greece and Rome. In modern times they are scattered throughout the west in far greater numbers than in the east. This prophecy must refer to an event that has not yet happened: God will supernaturally bring Israel from both east and west. The word translated *save* is the Hebrew word meaning to save spiritually or physically, usually the latter. This is no mere voluntary return on Israel's part. God is going to save her from the nations around her and bring her to Jerusalem.

The population of Jerusalem in modern Israel has grown dramatically, but it cannot compare with what God will do in the future. The Jewish people will dwell in the midst of Jerusalem. The Hebrew word for *to dwell* is also used in another form for the "tabernacle." The tabernacle was a symbol of God's dwelling place among his people. So the Jews will "dwell" in Jerusalem as God's chosen people. Furthermore, Jehovah will be their God in faithfulness and righteousness. The word *faithfulness* sometimes translated as *truth,* means to be found trustworthy. The word *righteousness* has a similar connotation. In that glorious day, Israel will learn that their Jehovah God is dependable, and as a result, they will be His people.

e. **Oracle #6: Reminder to the Remnant (8:9–13).** The application of this oracle to the people of Zechariah's day is clear. It is the people who were hearing in "those days" to whom it is addressed.

A contrast is being drawn between the desperate set of circumstances that prevailed when the exiles first returned and the much improved conditions in 518 B.C. God reminds them of the message of the prophets when the work of restoration of the temple was begun. Zechariah does not say which prophet he is referring to, but the only other prophet to minister during the rebuilding of the temple was Haggai, and the words of this section are similar to his. Haggai's written prophecy covers a period of only three months. He reminds the people of the paltry returns they had received for their labor and attributes it to their lack of faithfulness. Two years later, Zechariah says that his message is the same as Haggai's.

Things are different now (518 B.C.) than they were when the exiles returned (536 B.C.). That difference is stated in 8:10. (The history of this period is found in Ezra 2–4.) Opposition from the Gentile neighbors was intense and resulted in the stoppage of work on the temple. Zechariah reminds them that there was no real profit for their labor nor for that of their animals. Furthermore, there was constant harassment from those around them.

In both Zechariah and Haggai (2:17), God says that the problems the Jews experienced were designed to turn them back to Himself. But a new day has dawned for Israel, says the Lord (8:11). God's blessing will now rest on the returned community because, to a certain extent, they have turned to Him. Haggai promises the same thing (Hag. 2:19).

The land shall be prosperous because there will be a time of peace in which things can grow (seed of peace). The vine and the land in general will be fruitful because there will be adequate moisture. Furthermore, the returned remnant will be the recipient of this blessing (8:12).

The promise is expanded in 8:13 to include a removal of the

Deuteronomic curse, which was the consequence of disobedience (Deut. 28–30). In contrast, there will be a blessing.

The returning community of Jews was by no means a fully obedient one. Nehemiah and Ezra, as well as Haggai and Zechariah, were constantly confronting sin. The language of this passage, however, indicates that a substantial number of Jews were sufficiently obedient that God could turn chastisement into blessing. Again, the ultimate removal of the curse can only come in the Millennium, but, to some extent, it was lifted in Zechariah's time as the temple was nearing completion.

f. Oracle #7: God's Divine Purpose (8:14–17). God gives the reasons for His actions in 8:13–14. The Exile was the consummation of a long history of disobedience on the part of Israel. The ancestors of the present Jews had provoked Him to anger again and again, until He finally determined to bring disaster on them without mercy.

God has now brought His people back to the land. He has not capriciously changed His mind, but His purposes are being fulfilled as Israel has repented, and so He will bless Jerusalem and the house of Judah. These promises are designed to remove fear, to strengthen resolve in finishing the temple, and to encourage service and obedience to God.

The last two verses of the first segment of this chapter (8:16–17) summarize the previous verses about the conduct required of the people. Responsibility is always implicit in God's promises. The relationship between chapters 7 and 8 (the fasting question) has already been mentioned. God tells them in 7:8–11 what their fathers were supposed to do. Their refusal to obey brought devastating results. In 8:16–17 He tells the returned exiles what they are to do. In these two verses honesty and personal integrity are emphasized. *Truth* and *judgment* refer to a judicial attitude. As the community lives together, it is to be characterized by rectitude and justice in dealing with problems. The "judgment for peace" means right judicial decisions that result in peaceful living.

Furthermore, no one is to plan evil against his neighbor nor is he to give false testimony. God hates this way of life and puts great stress on truth (cf. Eph. 4:25 and Col. 3:9). Redeemed people, as the recipients of God's blessing, are obligated to live exemplary lives.

2. Second Segment: Millennial Promises (8:18–23)

The prophet now returns to the theme of fasts which began in chapter 7. The rebuke in chapter 7 for ritual without reality is now turned into a promise of blessing. The language of this segment cannot be related to Zechariah's day. It is the language of the future when God will supernaturally bring Israel back to the land for a thousand years of blessing under the rule of the Messiah (Rev. 20).

a. Oracle #8: Sorrow to Rejoicing (8:19). The fasts of sorrow will be turned into times of joy. The defeated and dejected people will become exultant. The Jews were keeping four fasts in connection with the fall of Jerusalem (see above, 7:4–7, for an explanation of the four fasts). This series of horrible events must have brought a deep sigh to every sensitive Jew. The promise that these fasts would become times of great joy and rejoicing must have been very encouraging. Still, God adds a word of admonition: Israel is charged to love truth and peace. These concepts are to be viewed as cause and effect (cf. 8:16); peace can only come from pursuing and obeying truth.

b. Oracle #9: The Transformation of the World (8:20–22). A recurring theme in the Old Testament is that God will bring the Gentile nations to Himself. In this age God is bringing Jew and Gentile into one body called the church (Eph. 2:11–13). This is happening even though the Jewish nation is set aside because of unbelief (Rom. 11:15). Therefore, the restoration of Israel will result in a greater work among the Gentiles than is now in progress, which is spoken of here in 8:20–23.

As the Jewish people turn to the Lord, the Gentiles will also be moved to seek Him. Many people and mighty nations shall seek the Lord of Hosts in Jerusalem and shall worship Him. Many apply this section to the church, but the language goes beyond the church age to that which is yet to come. What a marvelous time it will be!

c. Oracle #10: Primacy of Israel in the Salvation of Gentiles (8:23). This section is an amplification of the preceding one. The God-fearing Jewish man of that future day will be sought out by ten Gentiles who will ask for permission to follow him to Jerusalem. "We have heard that God is with you," they will say. People will recognize that the Jews of that time have a relationship with God. As a result, the Gentiles will want to identify with them and follow them to Jerusalem.

3. Summary

Chapter 8 is written to encourage the remnant of Zechariah's day to finish the task of building the temple and to live righteously. God encourages them by contrasting His blessing with the cursings of another day.

He also encourages them by giving them promises of the Millennium. The hope of the future should always be a stimulus for godly living. The believer during the church age should also be encouraged by the hope of God's work in the future (1 John 3:2–3).

For Further Study

1. Study Jeremiah 23:5,6 and Isaiah 11:1 for background on the "branch."

2. Read 2 Chronicles 26:16–23 to see what happened when a king tried to act as a priest. In light of that event, what do you believe is the significance of placing a crown on a priest?

3. Relate the "branch" of chapter 6 to the one in chapter 3. What conclusions can be reached about the identity of the branch?

4. If fasting was a proper practice in the Old Testament, why does Zechariah speak so strongly against the practice of the exiles? Should believers fast today? If so, what should be their attitude?

Part II

The Two Burdens
(Zechariah 9:1–14:21)

The First Burden

(Zechariah 9:1–11:17)

Chapter 9 begins the second section of the Book of Zechariah. The first section deals with the rebuilding of the temple and consists of visions and messages. This section of the book is of an entirely different nature. Through symbolic actions and apocalyptic visions, God reveals His plans for His people Israel.

The heading of chapter 9 is the Hebrew word that means a prophetic burden—usually a message of judgment that is difficult to bear and thus a burden. The twelfth chapter has "burden" as a heading, providing a two-part division. Consequently, the divisions will be titled "the first burden" (chapters 9–11) and "the second burden" (chapters 12–14).

The Second Burden (12:1–14:21)

The second burden repeats themes found in chapters 9 to 11 but with more intensity as the prophecy moves toward the climax of the establishment of God's kingdom "in that day."

Chapter 7

God's Victory in the World
(Zechariah 9:1–17)

Chapter 9 speaks of judgment and blessings on certain nations, but the problem is to determine when that judgment and blessing will take place. Does it refer to something that happened in the past, or is it to be viewed in an eschatological sense as something to occur in the future? Some of the things mentioned in 9:1–8 happened in the days of Alexander the Great in the fourth century before Christ. However, 9:7–8 sounds as though the Philistines will become proselytes to Judaism. Nothing is known in history of such an event. Yet, if the situation of 9:7–8 is eschatological, it is difficult to identify the Philistines in that future time, since the people now living in the coastal area of Israel are usually considered to be Arabs. However, these issues will be addressed as the chapter unfolds.

A. The People Judged (9:1–8)

1. The Northern Countries (9:1–4)

The Word of the Lord in this instance means that God has pronounced judgment against certain people. The first two towns mentioned are Hadrach and Damascus. Damascus is well known, but for many years no one had ever heard of Hadrach, and some commentaries have explained the word as if it were not a town but a description. Now, however, it is known to have been a town in Syria. It was mentioned in an Assyrian inscription as Hattarika, and it is probably the town mentioned in the Aramaic inscription of Zakir. Consequently, two towns in Syria—Hadrach and Damascus—are in view.

Speaking vividly, God says that His word of judgment began in the land of Hadrach and came to rest (lit., "its resting place") in the land of Damascus. Damascus was defeated by the Assyrians in 732 B.C., and when Alexander the Great came down the coast in his triumphant encounters with the Persian armies in the year 332 B.C., he conquered all of these areas mentioned. Zechariah, speaking from the fifth century B.C., is predicting the downfall of these people to the north, and the fulfillment probably took place in Alexander's time. Another interpretation is that Zechariah views all the attacks against these people over many centuries as typological of God's final victory over the nations.

A reason for this judgment is given at the end of 9:1. The NASB says, "For the eyes of men, especially of all the tribes of Israel, are toward the LORD." This is the easier reading. The more difficult reading is "the LORD has an eye on man and all the tribes of Israel," partly because of 9:8, "For now I have seen with my eyes." In addition, the eyes of the Lord "range to and fro throughout the earth" (4:10, cf. also 3:9). The word for *man* (adam) and the word for *Syria* (aram) are very similar in Hebrew, and some scholars think the *d* and the *r* were mixed up in the copying of the text. However, it would be better to leave it *adam*, referring to humanity in general as opposed to the tribes of Israel. Zechariah is saying that God has an eye on people and that His Word will be vindicated.

Additional cities to come under God's judgment are found in 9:2. Hamath is a city in southern Syria, which became the southernmost point in the Hittite treaty between Egypt and the Hittites in 1288 B.C. It occurs in the Books of Kings as a boundary city. "From the entrance of Hamath" is a phrase used quite often in connection with the kingdom of Israel (cf. 1 Kings 8:65).

Tyre and Sidon are very famous Phoenician cities. The Phoenicians were originally Canaanites whom the Greeks called "purple people" or Phoenicians. Sidon was the older city, and Tyre was built later as a fortress on a small island near the mainland. The Semitic word for rock is *tsur*, which the Greeks pronounced Tyre. The Phoenicians developed colonies in North Africa and battled the Greeks for control of the Mediterranean. Through their extensive trade, the Phoenicians became fabulously wealthy (as the text says in 9:2) and built up a formidable navy. The Assyrians spent five years trying to conquer Tyre without success. The Babylonians were unsuccessful after thirteen years of siege. Under Alexander, however, a causeway was built from the mainland, and Tyre was conquered in seven short months. The strategy was brilliant, and the conquest complete. This may be what Zechariah means when he says, "Behold the LORD will dispossess her and cast her wealth into the sea; and she will be consumed by fire" (9:4). God's great judgment came even though Tyre built a fortress and piled up silver like dust.

2. The Coastal Countries (9:5–8)

Alexander followed the normal invasion route for Palestine along the Mediterranean coast. Consequently, the next cities to be mentioned are the Philistine coastal cities. Only four of the five cities are listed here: Ashkelon, Gaza, Ekron, and Ashdod.

Ashkelon will see the destruction of Tyre and fear (9:5). Gaza, too, will tremble greatly, as will Ekron because her misplaced trust will disappoint her. While Ashkelon and Ekron are not mentioned in the extrabiblical histories, it is said that Gaza, depending on Arabian mercenaries and resisting desperately, was still defeated. "And a mongrel race will dwell in Ashdod." The word mongrel (KJV, bastard) is used elsewhere only in Deuteronomy 23:3, which says that such a person is not to enter the assembly of Israel. Here in Zechariah, the word is best translated "a mixed race." The Philistines will mix with other people, perhaps Jews, and will lose their proud racial independence.

Ashkelon will not be inhabited. The Romans built a town near the ancient site and called it Ashkelon. The Israelis have also built a town nearby with the same name, but only a salt encrusted mound remains of the ancient Philistine town called Ashkelon.

The most difficult part of the prophecy is found in 9:7. This verse indicates a conversion of the Philistines to the true worship of the Lord. Removing the blood from their mouths refers to the elimination of their idolatrous sacrifices, and the "detestable things" refers to pagan practices. Furthermore, Ashkelon will become a people who belong to the Lord, and they will be like a clan in Judah, which means that they will be treated as if they were native Judaeans. Ekron will be looked upon as the Jebusite. The analogy must refer to the fact that the pagan Jebusites were defeated by David and later became a part of Israel. Precisely where they stood spiritually is not clear. Second Samuel 24:18 tells us that Araunah the Jebusite sold his threshing floor to David for an altar site, but this does not tell us anything about his own devotion to the Lord. Whatever the Jebusites' spiritual state, they became a part of Israel, and that seems to be the indication about Ekron. When this happened is not clear from history. The name Philistine is not applied to a people after the Maccabean period, so they may have become assimilated into the Jewish people and adopted the Jewish faith. It may also be a typological reference to the future conversion to the Lord of the people of that area.

Ashdod was called Azotus in New Testament times. Phillip found himself in Azotus after his encounter with the Ethiopian eunuch, and the Bible says, "as he passed through he kept preaching the gospel to all the cities, until he came to Caesarea" (Acts 8:40). Whoever the inhabitants of Ashdod were by that time, they received the gospel.

If it is correct to assign the fulfillment of the prophecy of 9:1–7 to the time of Alexander the Great, one must ask how 9:8 fits that period, "But I will camp around my house because of an army." Alexander passed Jerusalem going to and returning from Egypt. Josephus even says that the high priest met him with the predictions of the Book of Daniel about Alexander (Dan. 8), and that Alexander was favorably disposed toward the Jews (*Ant.* 11.8.4–5). Without debating the authenticity of Josephus' statement, it can at least be said that the Jewish people were well-treated by Alexander, and the temple was not molested. Even during the dark days of Antiochus Epiphanes, though the temple was desecrated, it was not destroyed. As with the rest of this oracle, however, this may be a statement of the eschatological future when God will completely protect His people Israel.

"I will encamp around My house" (9:8) probably refers to

the temple, which by Alexander's time would have been in existence for almost two hundred years, but it also refers to the people for whose sake it exists. The word *oppressor* is used for a taskmaster over slaves (cf. Job 3:18). This is not a promise that the Jews will never have trouble again, but that they will be able to maintain a measure of independence. God's work on behalf of His people the Jews will be brought to a consummation in that future period called the Day of the Lord. That marvelous work resulting in the redemption of the physical seed of Abraham will come to pass through the astounding promise of 9:9–17.

3. Summary

The first eight verses of this chapter refer to God's judgment and blessing on the Gentile peoples. They may have some reference to Alexander's conquest of the Syro-Palestine cities in 332 B.C. The statement about a conversion of some of the Philistine people and God's protection of His people during those perilous times may refer to events of 300 B.C. to A.D. 100, although it certainly foreshadows God's eschatological work among the people of this area. Apparently, many of the Philistines were assimilated into Judaism, and some received the gospel from Phillip in New Testament times.

B. The Coming Messiah (9:9–17)

A period of judgment and blessing on the Gentiles and triumph and peace for Israel is predicted in 9:1–8, but this period is to be brought by a coming king. The poetic structure of the next verses is very beautiful.

> Rejoice greatly, O daughter of Zion!
> Shout in triumph, O daughter of Jerusalem!
> Behold, your king is coming to you;
> He is just and endowed with salvation,
> Humble, and mounted on a donkey,
> Even on a colt, the foal of a donkey.

All four gospels give the account of Jesus riding into Jerusalem on the back of a donkey. Both Matthew (21:1–7) and John (12:14–15) indicate that his action is a fulfillment of the prophecy in Zechariah. A harmony of the accounts indicates that they brought both the dam and her colt and that Jesus rode the colt. Zechariah 9:9 should then be considered messianic without any doubt.

The means for the future deliverance of Israel are through this promised king. Because of the greatness of this promise, the Jews are admonished to rejoice exceedingly. Daughter of Zion really means daughter Zion, that is, Israel. Daughter Jerusalem means the same thing. They are to rejoice because of what is going to come to pass.

1. The Characteristics of the Messiah (9:9)

The coming king has certain identifying traits. First, He is just. The word *just* in Hebrew means a right relationship with God and man so that one's conduct and actions are properly aligned with the righteousness of God. A primary function of a king is to administer justice; therefore, it is essential that a king be just in all his dealings (Isa. 11). Second, the king is also one who bears salvation. The form here is passive voice in the Hebrew. It would normally be translated "he is saved," or "delivered." Certainly, the king-messiah will be delivered by God, but the meaning here is probably better understood as "bearing salvation" or "endowed with salvation." That is, the coming Messiah will bring salvation—physically and spiritually. A third characteristic of the coming king is that He is humble. The word translated "humble" has a range of meanings in Hebrew that includes "poor" and "afflicted," as well as "humble." There has been much debate about whether riding on a donkey was a symbol of humility or greatness. In New Testament times, a great leader would have ridden on a horse or in a chariot. It is doubtful that the donkey represents either humility or greatness, but rather was simply a common method of conveyance. In any event, the Messiah comes into Jerusalem without the normal pomp of a triumphal monarch, but in the power of God.

2. The Work of the Messiah (9:10)

The verb shifts to the first person in 9:10. God is speaking, but He speaks as one who will be working through the Messiah. The instruments of warfare—chariot, horse and bow—will be cut off from Ephraim and Jerusalem. Ephraim, as the chief tribe in the northern confederation (Israel), became the name of the northern kingdom. In this prophecy, God sees all Israel restored and the removal of weapons of war, not because they are being forcibly removed, but because God will have given such victories that they will no longer be needed. Furthermore, the Messiah will speak peace to the nations (9:10), which means that when the Messiah establishes His kingdom, there will be peace with the nations around Jerusalem. The Messiah will bring peace and arbitrate peace.

The rule of the Messiah will be from sea to sea and from the river (Euphrates) to the ends of the earth. While some see this extensive rule as an exaggeration of the rule of the Jewish people during the Maccabean period, a normal sense would demand that it refer to the Millennium when Christ is ruling over the whole earth.

3. *The Deliverance of the Messiah (9:11–17)*

In that case, the freeing of the prisoners (9:11) should also indicate an eschatological fulfillment. These "prisoners of hope" are told to return to the fortified place (apparently an allusion to the land of Palestine). God promises to give them a double blessing when He brings them back to the land.

If the events of 9:10–12 are to be viewed eschatologically, there is a problem with the mention of the Greeks in 9:13. This verse promises that God will accomplish a great victory through Judah and Ephraim. He will "draw his string" with Judah and "fill his bow" with Ephraim. As God moves into battle "armed" with His people Israel, He will also stir up the sons of Zion against the sons of Greece.

The only time historically in which the Jews fought the Greeks was during the Maccabean period (c. 175–135 B.C.). The Greek kingdom, known as the Seleucid Dynasty, was ruling Syria. Under Antiochus IV (Epiphanes), the Jews were pressured to conform to the Greek religion. While a number of Jews were willing to go along with the program, a rebellion broke out that was led by the Hasmonaean family (Mattathias and his sons, the most famous of which was Judas Maccabaeus, called "the hammer"). Information for this period is found in Daniel 11:1–35; the Books of Maccabees, and Josephus' *Antiquities of the Jews.*

This passage should probably be understood as a reference

to the Maccabean period. Verses 14–17 speak of God giving the victory to the partisans of the Law. Similar language is used in Daniel 11 about those Jews who remained faithful to the Lord and His Law even during a time of great apostasy. The last part of 9:15 describes a bloody but victorious people. God's people are then called jewels in His crown, beautiful people who flourish under the blessing of God (9:16–17).

Even though this section depicts God's protection of His people during the Maccabean period, it also prefigures the Great Tribulation and the Millennium to follow. During this time, the Lord will fight for His people and give them victory over all their enemies. The Millennium is the ultimate triumph of the Lord over those who rebel against Him.

4. Summary

This interpretation of 9:9–17 means that three periods of time are predicted: the coming of Christ (with no distinction between His suffering and glory); the victory of the Jews during the Maccabean Period as a type of final victory; and the millennial reign of Christ in the eschatological future.

God gave revelation to the Old Testament prophets that was not always in chronological order. The Jews struggled, for example, with the fact that the coming Messiah would both suffer and have a glorious reign. Consequently, the early Jewish community had two messiahs: one who would suffer and one who would reign. This chapter is a classical illustration of that chronological mixture of prophecy that views the future as one continuous whole, when in actuality several events covering centuries are telescoped into one chapter and not always chronologically.

For Further Study

1. Look up the word *burden* in a concordance and see how it is used in the Old Testament.

2. Locate each city in 9:2–10 on a Bible atlas.

3. Read the accounts in the Gospels of Jesus riding into Jerusalem and answer the question: "How does the prophecy of one riding on a donkey fit this chapter?"

Chapter 8

The Regathering of Israel
(Zechariah 10:1–12)

The opening verses of chapter 10 are concerned with the same subject with which chapter 9 closed. The productivity of the land can only be assured with rain. God, through the centuries, taught Israel to trust Him for the rain and to expect the rains to be withheld if they were disobedient. He is talking about the same thing here. The rains are usually called the former and latter rains (Deut. 11:14; Hos. 6:3; Joel 2:23). The former rains come in autumn; the latter rains, in the spring. If Israel will only pray to the true God, He will send showers of rain on the fields.

A. The True Source of Rain (10:1–2)

The supply of rain for Israel was always tenuous. Egypt received her water from the Nile River, which flooded annually because of the melting snow in the African mountains. The land was irrigated from the Nile, and so a fairly consistent supply of water was usually available. The Israelites, on the other hand, depended on the Mediterranean Sea. The waters were carried by the clouds and dumped as they arose to clear the mountains of central Palestine. As a result water was rather inconsistent, and the Jews were very conscious of their dependence on God to bring it.

Some Jews, however, following the native Canaanite practices, were enticed to pray to the teraphim (idols), or to consult the diviners (people who used pagan practices to consult their gods). The prohibition against consulting idols is reminiscent of Jeremiah and proves that not all idolatry had ceased in Zecha-

83

riah's time. Before the Exile, there was a constant confrontation between Baal, the storm god, and Jehovah. This was the situation in Elijah's day (1 Kings 18). Jehovah declared Himself to be the Lord of all the earth by bringing a drought for three years. Baal, in the Canaanite pantheon, was the god of storms and rain. He was supposed to be able to bring rain. It became clear on Mount Carmel that Baal was unable to bring rain, whereas Jehovah brought it in response to Elijah's prayer. Jeremiah also argued that it was Jehovah alone who brought rain (14:22) He was speaking in a time of drought and trying to turn the people to the Lord.

Some people of Zechariah's day had failed to learn this important lesson. In spite of the fact that most Jews gave up polytheism in the Exile, some still clung to the native beliefs. One has to wonder whether these are Jews who did not go to Babylon but stayed in Palestine and never fully renounced their pagan practices.

Teraphim are mentioned as early as Genesis 31:30 when Rachel had stolen her father's teraphim. Laban calls them "gods." Precisely how they fit in the religious system is not clear, but apparently they were consulted in an effort to bring rain. However, the teraphim speak iniquity (KJV, *vanity*, 10:2). That is, since they cannot speak truth, everything they say is false and therefore sinful. The parallel line says the same thing about diviners. What these professional fortune tellers claim to "see" is false. Any such system (e.g., modern-day astrology) can only mislead. In Zechariah's day, those who had dreams or claimed to have them were speaking falsely. They comforted people in their distress, but it was an empty comfort.

B. The Leadership of the Flock (10:3–4)

Any time the Israelites pursued false gods, there was only one result: God judged them. In Zechariah's time also, the people wandered like a flock and were deeply afflicted because they had no true shepherd. The word *wander* usually means to move on from place to place (as Abraham moved toward the Negeb, Gen. 13:3). Here it refers to the random movement of sheep, who, without proper leadership, will always get into trouble (10:2). This situation is reminiscent of Jesus' reaction in the Gospels: "And seeing the multitudes, he felt compassion for them, because they were distressed and downcast like sheep without a shepherd" (Matt. 9:36).

Zechariah reminds the Jews why they are in trouble: The leaders were spiritually corrupt (see 1:12). Jeremiah 23 is an important commentary on this subject. In Jeremiah's day God was angry at the leaders (probably including King Jehoiakim) for scattering Israel. But He promised to regather His people from the places they were scattered (23:3–4), and in 23:5–8 Jeremiah speaks of the one great shepherd whom God will raise up over Israel and through whom He will lead the Jews back home. Zechariah probably has Jeremiah's great prophecy in mind as he speaks of the Jews of his day as scattered, afflicted sheep without a leader.

1. God's Anger against the Leaders (10:3)

Israel had no good shepherd, but there were plenty of bad ones, and God says that He has a case against them. The bad shepherds of Jeremiah 23 referred to the national leaders, but these bad shepherds are foreign rulers who mistreat the Jews.

The phrase "male goats" is a metaphor for leaders (cf. Isa. 14.9, Ezek. 34:17). God is not going to allow leaders to get away with misdeeds forever. He is angry, and He is going to punish them. The word for *punish* is the same as the one for *visit* and means to examine and then to treat well or badly depending on the situation. In this context, God is going to be harsh with the leaders because of their failure to look after the flock.

On the other hand, God will examine His own flock and treat it well. The title "Jehovah of hosts" appears again—the One who is able to do what He promises. The flock is specified here to be the house of Judah. The NASB says the Lord "has visited," but the translation should be "he will visit." In that day He will appoint His meek, afflicted flock as His majestic horse in battle. As the military commander rides his ornately harnessed horse at the head of his troops, so God will equip and use Judah to punish those nations who have abused her.

2. The New Leadership (10:4)

Having shown His displeasure toward the bad leaders, God now speaks about the good leadership He is going to raise up. The first issue in the passage is the question of the source of this leadership. The NASB says, "From them . . . ," that is, from Judah. The KJV says, "Out of him . . . ," that is, out of God. The Hebrew word is singular and therefore could refer to Judah as a single group of people, (NASB) or to God as the One who brings forth this leadership (KJV) . The KJV is better. God is the source of this leadership.

The next issue is the identification of the leadership. The prophecy probably has reference to any and all good leaders whom God will raise up over His people (cf. Jer. 23:4, where God promises to raise up shepherds who will take good care of the people). This general reference is supported by the fact that the fourth symbol (every ruler) is plural. At the same time, this entire section has an eschatological flavor, which looks to the time when God will raise up the leader *par excellence*, namely the Messiah. The following items, therefore, also characterize the rule of the Messiah.

a. The Cornerstone. The most significant occurrence of the word *cornerstone* is found in Isaiah 28:16, a passage cited by the Lord in Matthew 21:42 and by Peter in Acts 4:11 and 1 Peter 2:4–8. The cornerstone determines the angles of the walls and therefore is a stabilizing factor in a building. Jesus is the chief cornerstone who was rejected by the builders as being unsatisfactory but was chosen by God to be the foundation of His new building, the church.

b. The Tent Peg. The most common meaning of this word is "tent peg," as in the NASB. Sometimes it means "nail" as in the KJV. Isaiah 22:22–24 is a vivid prophecy of the replacement of an unfaithful steward (Shebna) with a faithful one (Eliakim). God says that Eliakim will be fastened as a nail in a sure place, that is, a peg on which things can be hung. His rule will be established, and people will have confidence in it. Likewise, the tent peg or nail in this context refers to the establishment of the kingdom and the effectiveness of the rule of the future shepherd.

c. The Battle Bow. The military aspect of the future ruler is given under the symbol of the bow. This coming one will be a mighty warrior who will lead His people to victory (cf. Isa. 63:2–4 and Rev. 19:11–16).

d. Every Ruler. The word *ruler* usually has a bad sense as in "oppressors" (KJV), but it seems to be positive in Isaiah 60:17, and so it could mean simply "rulers" in this context (NASB). The words *all* and *together* indicate more than one ruler. This phrase indicates that all good leadership comes from God, including the ultimate leader, the Messiah.

C. God's Victory through Israel (10:5–6)

Zechariah says that God will supernaturally bring a great victory through Israel. "Mighty men" (10:5) are the normal words for powerful soldiers. As soldiers they will fight, and God will be with them. They will defeat men on horseback. Both Judah and Joseph are involved. Judah, of course, represents the southern kingdom; Joseph, the northern kingdom. The northern kingdom is often referred to as Ephraim (Joseph's son), as in the next verse, because Ephraim was the largest tribe. It is referred to here as Joseph possibly to say that the original favor bestowed on Joseph will be given at this time also.

When will this mighty battle take place? Some commentators believe it fits well into the Maccabean Period (175–134 B.C.), but the tenor of the chapter, as already indicated, seems to indicate the last times. It is a time when the whole nation is represented (Judah, and Joseph, or Ephraim) and therefore refers to the Tribulation.

D. God's Return of Israel (10:6–11)

1. The Return (10:6)

The Hebrew word translated "and I shall bring them back" is an unusual form. It seems to be a combination of two roots: "to dwell" and "to return." The KJV gives a double translation with "and I will *bring* them again to *place* them." The NASB is correct in translating "and I shall bring them back," for the context indicates a restoration of Israel to her land. Their condition will be so good that it will be as if they had never been exiled. The first major scattering took place in 722 B.C. when Israel was deported by Assyria and the second was in 586 B.C. when Babylon exiled many Judaeans. The Romans deported many Jews in A.D. 70 and in A.D. 132. There were many minor deportations throughout history.

2. The Time of the Return

This return will take place sometime toward the end of the age, probably during the Tribulation. At that time, there will be a miraculous regathering of Jews from all over the world. The present state of Israel, while a marvelous example of God's preservation of the Jewish people, is not the fulfillment of this prophecy. Jehovah's own name is at stake, and He will answer the prayers of the Jews in that day.

3. The Place of Ephraim (10:7)

The mention of Ephraim (10:7) reinforces the fact that this prophecy refers to the last time when the northern and southern kingdoms will be reunited. Ephraim will act as a mighty soldier, and she and her children will rejoice when she sees what God is doing. The spiritual state of the Jews is indicated by the fact that they will trust in Jehovah.

4. The Nature of the Return (10:8–9)

The return of Israel will be supernatural, for God will whistle for them at that time (10:8). The return of Israel is spoken of in terms of redemption, both spiritually and physically. As God redeemed them from Egypt, so He will redeem them in the future. When He delivers them and brings them to their land, they will be as numerous as before.

Some commentators want to change the *sowing* of 10:9 to *scattering* (similar in the Hebrew), but the sowing indicates a providential good underlying an apparent catastrophe, that is, God scattered Israel in judgment, but that scattering results in Israel turning to God. Therefore, He was "sowing" them so that they could produce fruit. The Greek-speaking Jews called this in New Testament days the *Diaspora* or the *sowing*. It was to this *Diaspora* that Paul preached the gospel throughout Asia Minor.

Even though He sowed Israel among the peoples, they will remember Him in distant places and along with their children, will revive with hope and return to the land of Israel.

5. The Geography of the Return (10:10)

The geographical locations from which Israel will be returned are given in 10:10. Both Egypt and Assyria are mentioned. In Zechariah's time, Persia, not Assyria, was dominant. Nevertheless, the *land* of Assyria was still there, and it is in the modern countries of Iraq and Iran. Likewise, a large Jewish community continued to exist in Babylon for centuries (the famous Babylonian Talmud comes from there). At this writing there are few Jews in Egypt, and many have fled the persecutions of Iran and Iraq. Still, these two ancient population centers of Jewish people are places from which the Jews will be returned.

Israel will be brought back to Lebanon and Gilead (10:10). Southern Lebanon and Gilead were very fertile areas, but they were also very vulnerable to attack. Many Jews were deported from these places. Consequently, they will be brought back to these two areas, although that is not to say that they will not come to the rest of the country. "Until no *room* can be found for them" is saying that those areas will be fully repopulated by Jewish people.

E. God's Deliverance of Israel from Assyria and Egypt (10:11–12)

The following verses relate the exodus of the Jews from Egypt to God's future deliverance. The redemption of Israel by blood and their deliverance from Egypt is a cornerstone in Old Testament theology. The Jews were always reminding themselves, or God was reminding them, of that great event. Now, as God directs their eyes to the future, He uses language reminiscent of their deliverance from the bondage of Egypt.

God will cross over the sea of distress (10:11). Then He will strike the waves in the sea and finally the depths of the Nile will dry up. Just as God supernaturally brought Israel out of Egypt, performing miracle after miracle, He will do so again in that day. God's judgment will be upon Assyria, and her pride will be brought down. The power of Egypt will be broken for "the scepter of Egypt will depart."

F. Summary

Israel has been treated badly by the "shepherds" of the world for over two millennia. Yet, God in his protective care will raise up leaders to deliver them; indeed, He will raise up *the* leader, the Messiah, who will triumphantly bring them victory over the nations. They will then be restored to their land and know the blessing of the Lord in their lives.

God always looks after His own. That has been the message of the book to this point. God's children of this age can rejoice that a compassionate God sent His son to be the Good Shepherd who gave His life for the sheep. Having gone to such great lengths to redeem believers, He will not let them down in the days ahead.

For Further Study

1. Read Jeremiah 23:1–4. Why does God put such stress on shepherds? What are the implications of that emphasis for leadership in the church?

2. Read 10:5–12 carefully. What does the ordinary meaning of these words indicate about the return of the nation of Israel? How do you relate this promise to the modern state of Israel?

3. Locate Assyria and Egypt on a Bible atlas. How should we understand the reference to these countries in the twentieth century?

Chapter 9

The Shepherd and the Sheep
(Zechariah 11:1–17)

So far the first "burden" has presented the coming of the Messiah (9:9) with the glorious results for Israel (9:11–17) and the promise that Israel will return in great prosperity (10:3–12). In chapter 11, Zechariah prophesies that Israel will be judged for rejecting the shepherd.

A. God's Judgment (11:1–3)

The poetry of chapter 10 continues in 11:1–3, and these three verses form a conclusion to the unit in chapter 10. The mention of Gilead and Lebanon (10:10) as the places to which God will return His people leads to the discussion in 11:1–3 of the judgment of Lebanon, Bashan (Gilead), and Jordan. Commentators agree that 11:1–3 are speaking of the judgment of God, but it is difficult to determine who is being judged and when the judgment will be executed.

Some believe the trees are metaphors representing people, but it would be better to take them literally. Isaiah 37:24 shows that invading forces normally cut down choice trees to use in siege works. The language is dramatic, as the prophet personifies Lebanon and its trees. Lebanon is the area north of Israel, famous for her cedars. Even the modern flag of Lebanon has a cedar tree on its field. Lebanon is ordered to open her doors and allow a fire to enter and burn down the trees.

The cypress trees will also be damaged. This tree was common in the Middle East, though less important than the cedar. If the cedars have been destroyed (the glorious ones),

91

little hope is left for the cypresses. Likewise, the strong, stately oaks growing in Bashan (on the northeast side of the Jordan), are told to wail because the impenetrable forest (the cedars of Lebanon) has been cut down.

Two further items show the extent of the destruction. The shepherds are wailing because their glory is ruined. This statement probably refers literally to the shepherds and their flocks on the east of the Jordan whose pastures (glory) have been destroyed. Likewise, the pride of the Jordan is ruined. The pride of the Jordan refers to the thick growth on either side of the Jordan River, a favorite resort of lions. Consequently, when that forest is cut down the lions roar, since they have been robbed of their sanctuary.

Since the areas under discussion are the places to which the Lord will return His people, the conclusion must be that God is going to judge His people after their return to the land.

If the judgment will be on Israel as the people of God living in southern Lebanon, Bashan and around the Jordan, the second question asks when the judgment will take place. The context of chapter 10 speaks of the supernatural return of Israel to her land in prosperity. The context of chapter 11 refers to the rejection of the Shepherd of the flock. Verses 4–14 seem to be giving a reason for the judgment. C. H. Wright[1] is correct in saying that the language is general enough to refer to any siege of the land, but it is better to see that the judgment of 11:1–3 comes on Israel because of the rejection of the Shepherd. The time therefore is A.D. 70. Jesus' poignant words about Jerusalem are found in Matthew 23:37–39:

> O Jerusalem, Jerusalem, who kills the prophets and
> stones those who are sent to her!
> How often I wanted to gather your children together, the
> way a hen gathers her chicks under her wings,
> and you were unwilling.
>
> Behold, your house is being left to you desolate!
>
> For I say to you, from now on you shall not see Me
> until you say, "Blessed is He who comes
> in the name of the LORD!"

---

[1] C. H. Wright, *Zechariah and His Prophecies* (London: Hodder and Stoughton, 1879), pp. 302–03.

This prediction of a ruined temple leads the disciples to point out its marvelous construction. Jesus' response is that the temple will be destroyed.

Since the judgment on Israel is for rejecting the shepherd (fulfilled in the crucifixion of Christ), the time of the destruction of the land should be when the Romans besieged the city during the first revolt (A.D. 66–70), cut down much of its timber, and finally destroyed both the city and the temple.

B. The Shepherd's Commission (11:4–6)

This section is one of the most difficult in the book for it mentions specific times and events that cannot be identified with any certainty. There is no consensus among commentators, which should lend caution to the discussion. The conclusions that these are vivid symbolic depictions of events in the time of Christ's ministry on earth should be kept in mind.

The message of judgment in chapter 11 is in dramatic form. Whether Zechariah actually acted out any of this message before the people or simply stated it in message form is not clear, but it is stated in this dramatic form for emphasis.

Zechariah is first told to shepherd the flock of the slaughter, that is, a flock doomed to slaughter. This flock was being fattened for the meat market and pictures the destiny of God's people in the hands of careless shepherds.

The flock is in desperate need of a shepherd because those who buy the sheep slay them and go unpunished (lit. "they are not found guilty"). Likewise, those who sell them say, "Blessed be the LORD, for I have become rich!" Even their own shepherds have no pity on them (11:5). These shepherds, buyers, and sellers probably refer to foreign rulers who have oppressed Israel. Compare the similarity to chapter 1 where there is the lament that all the nations are at ease while Israel is still troubled. In terms of the time of Christ's ministry, it would refer to the Romans who were oppressing Israel.

God pronounces judgment in 11:6. Since the shepherds have no pity on the people, God will have no pity on the land. The land here is used in the sense of the earth in general, not simply the land of Israel. In this coming judgment, God will cause "the men to fall, each into another's power and into the power of his king." This depicts civil war and strife among Gentile nations. It is obviously divine retribution on those who are "killing" God's people and probably refers to the final great battle between God and the nations (Rev. 19).

C. The Shepherd's Activities (11:7–14)

Zechariah carried out his commission. He began to tend the flock (even the very poor flock). He took two staves for the task (cf. Ps. 23:4, "thy rod and thy staff"). Normally, these instruments were used to keep the sheep in order, but in this dramatic action, a significant name is given to each of the staves. One staff is called *favor*, a word which also means "pleasant" or "beautiful." The other is called *union* (lit. "ropes" or "bonds").

Next Zechariah "annihilates" three shepherds. The most perplexing problem of the chapter is the identification of these three shepherds. Some think they are three Gentile rulers who were cut off in a very short period of time (e.g., during the Maccabean period). However, beginning with 11:9, the entire nation of Israel is in view. It seems, therefore, that the three shepherds ought to be identified with Israel as well. However, nothing in history identifies these rulers. For this reason, many commentators interpret them as the termination of the three great offices in Israel at the time of Christ—Prophet, Priest, and King—but it is better to see the three shepherds as referring to Israel's leaders whom God has judged.

1. The Shepherd Rejects the Sheep (11:9–11)

Since the flock refuses the leadership of the shepherd, he rejects them. There comes a point in God's dealing with people when His patience is exhausted (the world, Gen. 6:1–3; the Canaanites, Gen. 15:16; Sodom and Gomorrah, Gen. 18–19; and Israel). The shepherd decides to "let nature take her course" against the flock: "What is to die, let it die; and what is to be annihilated, let it be annihilated; and let those who are left eat one another's flesh." How true this has been historically for the Jewish people and how tragic!

The second step in the rejection is the cutting in two of the staff "favor" (11:10). The "union " staff refers to the brotherhood of all Israel, and the "favor" staff represents the blessing of God upon Israel. When Naomi ("favor," "pleasant") returned from Moab, she said to the women of Bethlehem, "Do not call me Naomi ('pleasant'); call me Mara ('bitterness'), for the Almighty has dealt very bitterly with me" (Ruth 1:20). In the case of both Naomi and Israel, the word translated *favor* or *pleasant* means that God dealt with them favorably. The shepherd cuts in two the staff "favor" to indicate that God's blessing will no longer be on Israel. The cutting of the staff also represents the breaking of the covenant with the sheep. The "contract" was terminated. One should not read too much into the covenant here. Contrary to teaching that God is finished with Israel, it only means that the shepherd is going to bring judgment on the flock for rejecting Him. God's blessing will be absent from the flock. This idea is reinforced by the fact that the "union" staff will also be cut in two, indicating a disruption of the brotherhood of all Israel.

As the afflicted flock observes these actions, they discern that the judgment is from God. The "afflicted flock" may refer to a believing few in the nation. There are indications here and there in the Gospels and Acts that at least some of the leadership of Israel realized the significance of the rejection of Christ (cf. John 11:49–53; Acts 5:34-39).

2. The Shepherd's Pay (11:12–14)

The contract is broken, and the shepherd demands his pay, but puts the burden of response on the sheep (". . . but if not, never mind!"). As a result, the silver is weighed out and given to him. The amount is thirty pieces or shekels of silver. The people who hired him now place a value on his work. Thirty shekels was the payment required if an ox gored a male or female slave (Exod. 21:32). Thus did they value the shepherd's labor!

God responds to their offer contemptuously (11:13). He tells Zechariah to take the money and throw it to the potter. The sarcasm is heavy as the Lord says, "that magnificent price at which I was valued by them." Then Zechariah took the money and threw it to the potter in the temple (lit. "house of the Lord"). The identity of the potter has generated much debate. Some suggest changing the text to read *treasury* (a similar Hebrew word), but there is no textual evidence to justify it. It is more likely that a potter walked into the temple, and the money was tossed to him. There must have been several potters in any given town who were probably members of the lower class. In any event, the money was tossed to the potter as an amount so insignificant as to be treated as a tip.

Matthew relates this verse to the thirty shekels Judas was paid for betraying Christ (Matt. 27:1–9). The money was thrown in the temple, and the chief priests bought the potter's field with it as a burial place for strangers (thus the phrase "potter's field"). Near Jerusalem was a piece of land owned by a local pottery maker. The land was purchased and turned into a cemetery for unknown people or those without relatives.

Zechariah is not the only one who speaks of pottery. Jeremiah speaks of the great potter and the clay in chapter 18. Matthew is referring primarily to the Zechariah passage, but he may also be thinking of Jeremiah 18, and since Jeremiah is the better known prophet, he attributes the verse to him. Another possibility is that the prophet's name was abbreviated in Matthew's original text as ZROU (a common practice) and a later copyist read it as IROU (confusing the "Z" with an "I"—two similar-looking Greek capital letters). Matthew is giving the general sense of Zechariah 11:12–13.

The shepherd of Zechariah 11 is to be identified with Christ. He was rejected and valued as if an ox-gored slave. He then went to the Cross in fulfillment of the Father's plan of redemption, and Israel has been in a state of rejection since. The staff "favor" has been cut in two.

Finally, the second staff, "union," is cut in two. Union signifies the unity of the Jewish people. In the days of Christ, there was great disunity among the people of Israel. The nation was divided into Pharisees, Sadducees, Herodians, Zealots, Essenes, and other groups. To this day only the fact of Jewishness binds the people together. Beyond that there is great disunity.

D. The Wicked Shepherd (11:15–17)

1. The Wicked Shepherd Personified (11:15)

The imagery continues as God tells Zechariah to take the equipment of a foolish shepherd. The word translated *foolish* in

Hebrew does not mean merely silly; it means to be spiritually and morally foolish. This shepherd is not harmlessly foolish; he is diabolical in his intents and actions. A clear description of this type of shepherd is found in John 10, where Christ contrasts his own love and devotion to the flock with that of a hireling who "flees when the wolf comes."

2. The Wicked Shepherd's Acts (11:16)

This shepherd does two things that are equally devastating (11:16). On the one hand, he neglects the flock: He does not care for the perishing, (same word as *annihilate* in 11:8), does not seek the scattered (*to scatter* in Hebrew is translated *youth* in the KJV), does not heal the wounded or provide for the sheep. But as if this neglect were not criminal enough, the wicked shepherd also actively destroys the flock. He eats the plump sheep and tears off their hooves. He has only a selfish interest in the sheep.

This shepherd is obviously some very wicked person who will seek to destroy the people of Israel. Many people in history would fit that description, but a coming wicked ruler fits it in a horrifying way. Revelation 13 speaks of a "beast" coming up from the sea who will rule most of the world through Satan's power. This person is called "the Antichrist" because he is against all that Christ stands for and puts himself in the place of Christ. He will be active during the Great Tribulation. The nation of Israel, having rejected the true shepherd, will have to face the wicked one.

3. The Judgment of the Wicked Shepherd (11:17)

God will not abandon His people. The wicked shepherd will be destroyed as a sword strikes him on the arm and in the eye. The right arm symbolizes his power—it will be withered; the right eye symbolizes his intelligence—it will become blind. And so God will destroy the wicked shepherd (11:17) with the spirit of His mouth and the brightness of His coming (2 Thess. 2:8).

E. Summary

Chapter 9 predicts judgment on the coastal cities (vv. 1–8), the coming of Christ and His reign (vv. 9–10), and victory and glory for Israel (vv. 11–17). Chapter 10 speaks of God's ability to bring rain (vv. 1–2), His anger against bad leaders (v.3), His promise of good leaders and *the* good leader (vv. 4–5), and Israel's regathering in triumph (vv. 6–12). Chapter 11 refers to the time of Christ's rejection (vv. 4–14), the judgment of God upon Jerusalem as a consequence (vv. 1–4), and the coming Antichrist (vv. 15–17).

In a general way, this unit reminds believers that God is sovereignly ruling the world and world events. All history is moving toward the denouement of Christ's kingdom on earth as it is in heaven.

For Further Study

1. Compare this chapter with Jeremiah 23 where God speaks strongly about leadership. How can you explain how God allows His people to be "doomed for slaughter" when He also condemns the leadership?

2. Do you see any connection between the staff "union" and the two sticks of Ezekiel 37:15–28? Give reasons for your answer.

3. Compare the language of 11:17 with John 10. Whom does the "foolish" shepherd represent?

The Second Burden

(Zechariah 12:1–14:21)

Chapter 12 begins the second unit of Part II of Zechariah. "The burden of the word of the LORD concerning Israel" provides the heading for chapters 12–14.

The second burden repeats themes found in chapters 9–11 but with more intensity as the prophecy moves toward the climax of the establishment of God's kingdom "in that day."

Some of the most significant messianic passages of the Old Testament are found in this unit. The final chapter on the coming of Messiah is perhaps the most dramatic of the prophecies.

Chapter 10

Troubles and Deliverance for Judah
(Zechariah 12:1-14)

Both chapters 9 and 12 begin with a reference to the "word of the LORD": Chapter 9 directs it to the land of Hadrach; chapter 12, toward Israel. Chapter 9 speaks of the eyes of God being on man and all the tribes of Israel; chapter 12 speaks of opening the eyes of the Lord upon Judah.

The name Israel, as the covenant name of God's people, appears in the superscription, whereas Judah and Jerusalem appear throughout the rest of the chapter. In the postexilic period, Judah referred to the whole nation.

A. War and Victory in Jerusalem (12:1–9)

1. The Declaration of Jehovah (12:1–2)

God's ability to carry out His promises is shown by the statement that He stretches out the heavens, lays the foundation of the earth, and forms man's spirit within him. The great Creator of the universe and life within it is surely able to fulfill His Word in history (for the phrase, "stretch out the heavens," see Isa. 44:24; 51:13; Ps. 104:2; Job 9:8).

Chapter 12 opens with a siege against Jerusalem. All the nations are gathered against the city, and her situation seems hopeless. However, God will make Jerusalem a "cup that causes reeling to all the peoples around." The cup is the symbol of God's wrath, from which people are forced to drink (cf. for the simile, Jer. 25:15–28; 49:12; 51:7; Isa. 51:17, 22). The nations believe they can easily defeat Jerusalem, but God turns the city into a cup of anger that will control the nations as if they were drunkards.

The phrase "and when the siege is against Jerusalem, it will also be against Judah" is difficult. The NASB has gained the sense of the verse: Judah (the countryside) and Jerusalem (the city) will be united in the events of the last days.

2. *Jerusalem as a Damaging Stone (12:3–5)*

The imagery changes from the wine bowl of God's wrath to a heavy stone. The nations attack Jerusalem to maneuver her into their "political building," but instead of moving the stone, they become lacerated from the sharp edges. The word translated *injured* appears elsewhere only in Leviticus 19:28 and 21:5. There it refers to the pagan practice of cutting the flesh in a frenzy of idol worship. Here it is accidental cutting caused by lifting a sharp-edged stone. Jerusalem, far from being an easy prey to the nations, will be a source of consternation.

When the armies are gathered against Jerusalem, God's wrath will be demonstrated. Cavalry charges will be stopped as the horses become blinded, totally confused, and the riders become insane. The result will be pandemonium. In contrast to His judgment of the nations, God will "open his eyes upon Judah" (NASB, "watch over"). God's protection of His people in the face of imminent catastrophy is marvelous!

The protection of Jerusalem will provoke a response of praise from the inhabitants of the countryside. "Clans" (KJV, *governors*) are the loose family groupings within the tribes of Israel. The word can be translated *governor* or *prince* as it is in Genesis 36:15. Here, the NASB is probably correct in translating it as groups of people rather than leaders. The clans recognize that victory for their brothers in Jerusalem is a victory for them. They testify that the inhabitants of Jerusalem are a strong support for them through Jehovah of Hosts. Some have imagined a cleavage between the rural people (Judah) and the urban (Jerusalem), but this verse shows the people united in their testimony of praise to the Lord who gives deliverance.

3. Physical Deliverance of Jerusalem and Judah (12:6-9)

Besides the spiritual unity between the rural and urban people, God will use the clans of Judah to punish the invaders. They will become like a firepot among pieces of wood and a flaming torch among sheaves. The "firepot" refers to a portable bucket containing a fire. Positioned in the middle of wood, its intense heat sets the surrounding material on fire. The flaming torch among sheaves is illustrated by Samson who tied torches to the tails of foxes and turned them loose in the standing grain of the Philistines (Judg. 15:4–5). Likewise, Absalom set fire to Joab's field of barley (2 Sam. 14:30). In just such a devastating way, God will use Judah against the enemies of His people, and as He does, Jerusalem will also be protected and dwell in her place.

"The LORD also will save the tents of Judah first . . ." A contrast is being made again between Judah and Jerusalem. Tents may indicate a rural area as opposed to the city. The point is that Jerusalem as the capital will not be more prominent than the countryside.

The latter part of 12:7 states that God's purpose for Israel is unity and equality. The reason God will exalt Judah is to prevent the glory of the house of David and the inhabitants of Jerusalem from exceeding that of Judah. Whether in the countryside or city, God's people will have the same glory.

When the nations surround the city of Jerusalem, God will be a shield over her inhabitants. How beautiful is the imagery of a shield! A basic component of the weaponry of that day, the shield was indispensable to the warrior. God Himself will be the shield for the inhabitant of Jerusalem.

Not only will God be a shield, He will provide extra strength to His people. Even the weak stumbling one will be as David. David, because of his exploits as a youth and as a man, became the unequaled leader of the armies of Israel. When God delivers His people, even the weak one will be like David (cf. 1 Cor. 1:27–29).

The next step up is the house of David. The royal family will be strengthened by the Almighty in such a way that they are like God, indeed like the angel of God. The comparison with

God is fascinating. This statement is amplified by the phrase "like the angel of the LORD before them." The allusion is probably to the angel of His presence (Exod. 23:20–23) who delivered Israel from Egypt. The point is that supernatural endowment for the people of God will enable them to do exploits.

Finally, 12:9 indicates that God will destroy the nations who opposed Jerusalem. The phrase "set about" (NASB) means "to seek" not in the sense of attempting, but in the sense of actively pursuing. There will be a great judgment from God against these peoples who are set against the Jews.

The eschatological setting described in chapter 12 is the same as the Battle of Armageddon in Revelation 19. There the nations are gathered against Jerusalem, and God delivers a crushing blow against them to deliver His people. From Zechariah, it is clear that the human element (Judah and Jerusalem) will be used by the Almighty as He brings this great victory to pass.

B. Spiritual Deliverance for Judah and Jerusalem (12:10–14)

A marvelous event is depicted in these verses. As God destroys the enemies of the Jews, a very significant thing will happen to them. God will pour out on the house of David and the inhabitants of Jerusalem the spirit of grace and of supplication. In the phrase "spirit of" one must ask whether the spirit is a person (i.e., the Holy Spirit) or an attitude (e.g., the spirit of humility). Here it probably refers to the third person of the Trinity—the Holy Spirit who will produce favor and supplication. These latter two words have a common Hebrew base. Both refer to grace or graciousness. They mean "to become amenable to someone." The work of the Spirit will cause the people to turn to God with humility.

It is important to note that the people look kindly and with repentance on the one they pierced *after* the Spirit is poured out upon them. Therefore, God will convict the Jewish people and they will repent. Romans 11:26 indicates that God will be dealing with "all" Israel in that day in contrast to "part" Israel or the remnant in the church age.

This striking prophecy continues in verse 10: "So that they

will look on me whom they have pierced; and they will mourn for him, as one mourns for an only son." This verse is referred to twice in the New Testament: once concerning the crucifixion of Christ (John 19:37) and once referring to the return of Christ (Rev. 1:7). The word translated *pierced* occurs eleven times in the Old Testament and means to be thrust through with the sword, lance, or similar weapon. "They shall look on *me*" shows that it is Jehovah who will be pierced. A number of Hebrew manuscripts read "they shall look on *him*," which also occurs in John 19:37, but the "me" should be allowed to stand. It is Jehovah who is pierced in the person of Jesus Christ.

The mourning is one of repentance. The Jewish nation will become aware of their responsibility for the death of her Messiah, even though all humanity is guilty in the sense that their sins sent Him to the cross. Once under the conviction of God, they will mourn the death of their Savior and Messiah.

The national mourning of the Jews will be intensive like the mourning of Hadadrimmon in the plain of Megiddo. Hadad was the name of a pagan deity of the Canaanites, the storm god also known as Baal. Some suggest that this mourning was a very intense pagan festival held for him.

A more likely suggestion is that Hadadrimmon was a place near Megiddo. The Jews mourned greatly when young King Josiah was killed in battle on the plains of Megiddo trying to stop Egypt from going to the aid of Assyria. Jeremiah uttered a lament for him and a custom of mourning for him continued to the fifth century (2 Chron. 35:25). As people mourned in bitterness over the premature death of the valiant descendant of David, so they will mourn over the greater David who was killed carrying out His Father's mission.

Close people tend to mourn together. The Israelites in the wilderness, for example, wept by families—each man at the doorway of his tent (Num. 11:4–10). Something similar is involved here because groups of Israelites will be mourning together. The groups are these: the family of David, Nathan, Levi, Shimei, and all the remaining families. David and Nathan (a son of David) probably represent the royal family, and Levi and Shimei (a grandson of Levi) represent the priestly faction.

The Israelites will mourn in repentance over their crucified Messiah-Savior and the mourning will be by families.

C. Summary

Chapter 12 records that in the last days there will be a concerted attack against Jerusalem by the nations. However, in the midst of that attack, God will deliver the inhabitants of Jerusalem by supernatural means. Finally, there will be a national repentance as the Jews look on the pierced Lord Jesus Christ and mourn for Him.

This chapter is a statement of God's purposes in history. In spite of the confusion in the world today and the humanly insolvable problems, God is in charge of world events. In His time, He will set all things right. The Jewish people will be the centerpiece of His work as He judges the nations for their rebellion against Him and establishes His kingdom on earth.

For Further Study

1. Read Isaiah 40:1–31. Why is there such emphasis in Isaiah and Zechariah on the greatness of God? What are the implications of that greatness for the present age?

2. Look up the cross-references on the statement "they shall look on me whom they have pierced" and explain how the New Testament understands it.

3. Explain the mourning in this chapter in light of Revelation 1:7.

Chapter 11

Purification of Israel
(Zechariah 13:1–9)

The events of the last days continue into chapter 13. The sequence of events established in these two chapters is that God will pour out His Spirit upon Israel who will mourn over the one they pierced. Then a fountain will be opened for the house of David and for the inhabitants of Jerusalem. The fountain is to cleanse from sin and impurity. As in chapter 12, the house of David and the inhabitants of Jerusalem designate the whole nation.

A. The Opened Fountain (13:1)

God promises a fountain for cleansing. He will deal graciously with Israel by purifying her from sin. In 3:3–4 the filthy garments are removed from Joshua the high priest, who stands in the place of the nation of Israel—a removal that symbolizes the spiritual purification of the nation. The symbol used in chapter 13 is an open fountain to provide a bath of purification.

The fountain is opened to deal with sin and impurity. The Hebrew word for *sin* means to "miss the mark" (cf. Judg. 20:16 where the word is used literally for slinging a stone and not *missing*). The idea is that the people have missed the mark of holiness that God requires.

The second word *impurity* is less common. It is found in Leviticus in the sense of menstruation and the ceremonial uncleanness involved (Lev. 12:2, 5; 15:19–33). However, in Numbers 19:9–21 the "waters of purification" are used for general uncleanness, such as when a person touches a dead body. It is descriptive of the land of the Canaanites before the Israelites entered it (Ezra 9:11). Sinfulness and impurity shall be washed away in the fountain opened by the Lord.

A gushing fountain of water is a metaphor of all that is good. "The fear of the Lord is a fountain of life" (Prov. 14:27) and "They have forsaken me, the fountain of living waters" (Jer. 2:13). Israel's repentance will result in God's miraculous work of regeneration. The fulfillment of this promised fountain is the cross of Christ. John the Baptist pointed his disciples to Christ and said, "Look, the Lamb of God, who takes away the sin of the world!" (John 1:29). The appropriation of this promise by the *whole* nation of Israel will take place during the Tribulation.

B. The Removal of False Prophets (13:2–6)

Cleansing in the fountain results in the removal of false prophets from the land. Since false prophecy virtually ceased after the Exile, it is valid to ask when this will occur. The Scriptures indicate that some will arise in the last days and presume to speak in the name of the Lord (2 Thess. 2:4; 13:1). In the pre-exilic period, idolatry was Israel's most common sin. Jeremiah constantly pleads with Judah to put away her idols and turn to the Lord. The current resurgence of witchcraft and astrology shows that in any period of history such idolatrous practices are possible.

In that day, God will remove both the idols (the labor of men's hands) and the false prophets. In addition, the spirit of uncleanness will be removed. The spirit of grace and supplication is promised in 12:10 in contrast to the spirit of uncleanness in chapter 13. The unclean spirit leaving Israel but later returning is the subject of one of Jesus' parables (Matt. 12:43–45). In that future day of which Zechariah speaks, the unclean spirits will be removed permanently.

Those false prophets who are left will find that even their parents turn against them. Parental zeal will surpass even the requirements of the Law. While Deuteronomy 13:6–11 instructs relatives, including parents, to pronounce the death penalty on a false prophet, Zechariah says that the parents will kill the false prophet themselves.

Such zeal for the truth will remove the advantages of being a false prophet, so that each one will be "ashamed" of his vision when he prophesies. In their fear, they avoid actions that identify them as prophets. The prophets often wore special garments (2 Kings 1:8; Mark 1:6). In fear of their lives, these false prophets will no longer wear such garments. When challenged, a man will deny being a prophet (13:5) and claim to be a slave farmer, purchased as a youth by his owner.

The interrogator remains suspicious (13:6). He says, "What are these wounds between your arms?" (lit. "between your hands"). This mention of wounds and hands has led some commentators to conclude that the reference is to Christ. However, the entire context is a conversation with the man who is trying to prove that he is not a prophet. Furthermore, the wounds are *between* the hands, not *in* them. Between the hands (NASB, *arms*) is a Hebrew idiom for the chest (cf. 2 Kings 9:24). These are self-inflicted scourge marks. The false prophets whipped themselves into a frenzy as they worked up to their ecstatic state (1 Kings 18:28). This man has scars on his chest from such activity. In answer to the question, he says that he received them in the house of friends (loved ones). He claims that his relatives beat him and left the scars.

C. The Smitten Shepherd (13:7–9)

This section changes subjects and should be related to chapter 11, where shepherding is the theme. As in Isaiah 53, God redeems through the vicarious work of the servant. In chapter 12, God's chosen one was pierced. In this chapter, he is smitten. Israel must be saved through the smiting of the shepherd.

The sword (13:7) is personified. God addresses it and commands it to rise against His shepherd. This situation should be compared with Isaiah 53:4–6, where the people supposed that the smitten one received what he deserved. The rejoinder to that wrong conclusion was that "He was pierced through for our transgressions . . . the chastening for our well-being *fell* upon him." The death of Christ was the Father's will, even though He used human agency to accomplish it.

An outstanding fact is that the shepherd belongs to Jehovah.

As a matter of fact, He is the "man, my associate." This word is used otherwise only in Leviticus (6:2, 19:15, 17; 25:14, 15) where it means "companion," "neighbor," "friend." This shepherd bears a special relationship to Jehovah. Keil says,[1]

> The shepherd of Jehovah, whom the sword is to smite, is therefore no other than the Messiah, who is also identified with Jehovah in ch. xii. l0; or the good shepherd, who says of Himself, "I and my Father are one" (John x. 30).

In 13:7, the command becomes specific: "Strike the shepherd that the sheep may be scattered." The NASB has taken the scattering as the purpose, but it is more likely the result: "And the sheep will be scattered." This graphic portrayal is precisely what takes place when something happens to the caretaker of the sheep. Then the flock moves away in disorder. Even Jesus applied this verse to Himself at the Last Supper (Matt. 26:31). His prophecy was fulfilled when the disciples fled.

There is a promise for the flock: "And I will turn my hand," says the LORD, "against the little ones." God's hand not only turns in judgment but also in blessing. The fulfillment of this promise is the Tribulation, when Israel will undergo a time of trouble hitherto unknown (Matt. 24:21). Two-thirds will be cut off and die (13:8, the two-thirds probably should be taken as "majority"), and one third will be left. Then the remaining third will be tested as silver and gold (13:9), and the results will be glorious. Israel will call on the name of the Lord, and He will answer her. God will say, "Israel is my people," and Israel will say, "Jehovah is my God."

D. Summary

Chapter 13 predicts a fountain that is a symbol of purification (v.1). The purification of the nation of Israel will result in the removal of false prophets (vv. 2–6). Finally, the theme of the Good Shepherd is resumed (vv.7–9) with a prediction of His crucifixion and the scattering of the flock (the disciples). The nation of Israel will go through the Tribulation.

---

[1] Keil, *The Twelve Minor Prophets*, vol. 2 in *Biblical Commentary on the Old Testament*, p. 397.

Two-thirds will be killed, but one-third will be tested and proved to be God's children.

The sin problem, ever clouding the relationship between the Creator and His created ones, had to be solved by the vicarious suffering of one for the many. Our Lord Jesus Christ became flesh that He might suffer for His own. Israel nationally will one day accept that One as her Messiah and Savior. All believers need to rejoice because of the grace of God manifested through the pierced, smitten Good Shepherd.

For Further Study

1. Can you find any other teaching in the Old Testament about cleansing through water? How does it relate to this "opened fountain"?

2. Some believe the question "What are these wounds between your arms?" refers to the crucifixion marks of Christ. Read the context carefully and try to determine the one to whom the question applies.

3. Read the New Testament reference to 13:7. How is Matthew understanding the context of Zechariah 13?

Chapter 12

The Consummation
(Zechariah 14:1–21)

Chapter 14 predicts important events for the end of the age. It reiterates the fact of the nations coming against Jerusalem (cf. 12:10), Jehovah's supernatural intervention, Jehovah's reign in Jerusalem and the peace that accompanies that reign, Jehovah's judgment of the nations that have come against Jerusalem, and Jehovah's blessing on the remaining nations as they keep the festival of booths. The last three verses of chapter 13 are amplified in chapter 14.

A. Battle against Jerusalem (14:1–8)

A final battle where the nations are gathered against the city of Jerusalem is a recurring theme in both the Old and New Testaments (Ezek. 38; Dan. 9:24–27; Rev. 20:8–9). Some commentators struggle to allegorize this chapter to make it refer to the church, but literal interpretation demands that it refer to the nation of Israel and the city of Jerusalem.

1. Nations Gathered by God (14:1–2)

"Behold a day is coming for the LORD" means that a day is coming, as yet undesignated, that belongs to the Lord. The Bible speaks often of the Day of the Lord, meaning a time when God will set all things right through judgment and blessing. The chronology of the day is left indefinite. That the "day" belongs to the Lord indicates His sovereign control over the events in it. These verses show initial stages of the attack against Jerusalem.

The Gentile nations, probably sending representative

112

armies against the city, have been victorious. They are so confident of their superiority that they are dividing the spoil in the city itself rather than waiting to do so elsewhere (14:2). They may believe that it is their own strategy that has brought them there, but in reality it is a sovereign God who has engineered their attack as part of His overall plan for Israel.

The results are horrible. The bloodthirsty soldiers, having taken the city, first plunder the homes. Then they abuse the women—a characteristic act of victorious soldiers and one of the most frightening atrocities to a powerless people. Half of the city will go into exile. The Jews have often faced the horrors of exile! The first great exile from Jerusalem was in three stages (606, 597, 586 B.C.), during which Judah experienced what her sister Israel had undergone almost one hundred years earlier. Then, under the persecution of Antiochus Epiphanes (second century B.C.), the Jews of Jerusalem suffered greatly at the hands of her enemies. In A.D. 70, the Romans inflicted great ignominies upon the occupants of the city who had defied them for three years. A second revolt in A.D. 132 brought even worse consequences. Zechariah is predicting the doleful procession of captives struggling to keep a few belongings and as much dignity as possible moving to an unknown destination.

The other half of the people will not be cut off from the city. Cutting off normally has negative connotations (cf. Exod. 12:15). Therefore, not to be cut off from the city that contains the temple and the place of God's blessing should be seen as a blessing itself. They will not be separated from God; they will be the remnant—the believing group within Israel.

Time and again Israel has confronted superior forces. In the twentieth century, she struggles to survive in the midst of great hostility. The modern survival is looked upon with a certain pride in human accomplishment, but in that black hour, Israel will have only one place to turn.

2. The Lord Fights against the Nations (14:3)

The dramatic appearance of the Lord is portrayed in 14:3: "The LORD will go forth and fight against those nations as when He fights on a day of battle." The phrase "go forth" is used several times almost in a military sense (cf. 1 Kings 20:16–21).

Moses sang, "the Lord is a warrior" (Exod. 15:3). Isaiah 9:6 says that the Messiah is to be called a "mighty God" (lit. a "warrior God"). In that day, God will go forth in behalf of Israel as a great warrior.

3. The Geological Changes in Olivet (14:4)

A phenomenon will take place when the Lord returns. His feet will touch the Mount of Olives from which He ascended into heaven (Acts 1:9–11), and there will be a great cleavage. The rest of the Jews left in the city will be in continued fear because of the enemy nations and possibly because of the earthquake activity associated with the cleavage of Mount Olivet.

East of Jerusalem lies the deep Kidron Valley. Next to the valley is a high, steep mountain called the Mount of Olives. David fled from Absalom by climbing this mountain (2 Sam. 15:30) and making his way to the Jordan. God will divide the Mount of Olives in two and create a new valley running east and west through which the Jews may flee. This geological reordering will bring about other changes discussed later.

4. The Fleeing Jews (14:5)

The Jews in Jerusalem, seeing this newly opened valley will flee the city to the east. "My mountains" refers to the two mountains created by God in separating the Mount of Olives. The earthquake in the time of Uzziah is not mentioned in the historical books (but cf. Amos 1:1). Earthquakes, however, were fairly common in that area, and the one in Uzziah's time must have been quite significant.

The new valley extends to Azel. The Hebrew *Azel* also means "beside" or "near," and some have suggested that it should be so translated here. However, it is more likely the name of a place. The phrase is similar to Joshua 3:16: "The waters which were flowing down from above stood and rose up in one heap, a great distance away at Adam." Azel is probably a now-unknown village east of Jerusalem. The Jews will flee through this newly opened corridor to safety.

"Then the Lord, my God, will come, *and* all the holy ones with Him!" What a glorious statement. All suffering and sin will fade into the past with the glorious, personal appearance of the One who left His bewildered disciples on the summit of Mount Olivet in the first century. He will be accompanied by the holy ones. This phrase usually refers to angels in the Old Testament, but New Testament revelation includes saints who have gone to be with the Lord (1 Thess. 3:13).

5. Astronomical Changes (14:6–7)

The heavenly bodies will also undergo miraculous changes. There will be no light (cf. Isa. 13:10; Joel 3:15; Amos 5:18; Matt. 24:29). The second part of 14:6 is very difficult because of the obscure Hebrew. It says literally: "The honorable ones shall be concealed." Since the parallel line says that there will be no light, it is best to see in this line something about the diminishing of the heavenly luminaries. The period of the Lord's return will be unique because there will be supernatural light even though the natural light has been diminished (14:7). The KJV says it will be "one" day. The Hebrew word *one* means in this passage "one of a kind" or "unique." In spite of the absence of the natural sunlight, there will be light, but it will be supernatural. This unique day is known to the Lord because He has especially planned it.

6. New River (14:8)

In addition to the other phenomena, there will also be a flowing river. Water in the Middle East is more appreciated than in the West because of its scarcity. Springs were very precious. When the Lord comes to earth, flowing waters (lit. "living waters") will originate in the city of Jerusalem and flow in two directions. Half of the water will flow to the eastern sea or the Dead Sea, and the other half will flow to the western sea or the Mediterranean Sea. Furthermore, this water will not diminish in the summer as with most streams. It will provide its refreshing sustenance year-round.

B. The Lord Reigns—Peace in Jerusalem (14:9–11)

God promised David that he would have a descendant to sit on His throne forever (2 Sam. 7:12–16). When Gabriel spoke to Mary about her son, he said,

He will be great, and will be called the Son of the Most High;
and the LORD God will give him the throne of his father,
David; and he will reign over the house of Jacob forever; and
his kingdom will have no end (Luke 1:32–33).

The fulfillment of those Davidic promises is found in the
statement that "Jehovah will be king over all the earth." This
verse speaks of the millennial reign of Christ—the messianic
era longed for by all godly Jews. The warp and woof of the Old
Testament is that God will bring in a time of unprecedented
blessing to the earth. This promise should not be spiritualized;
it is literal. Although the concept occurs throughout the Old
Testament, the time frame of one thousand years is given for it
only in Revelation 20.

Not only will Jehovah be king, He will be "one Jehovah"
and "his name shall be one." This use of the word translated *one*
should be compared with the same word in 14:7, where it was
translated *unique.* The meaning is similar here. Jehovah will be
the only one, and His name the only one. This declaration is an
echo of the famous "Shema" of Deuteronomy 6:4: "Hear, O
Israel, the LORD our God is one LORD." There is no God except
Jehovah. In that day all will confess to the truth of this
statement. As Paul says in Philippians 2:10–11,

that at the name of Jesus every knee should bow, of those who
are in heaven, and on earth, and under the earth, and that
every tongue should confess that Jesus Christ is LORD, to the
glory of God the Father.

When the Lord personally reigns in Jerusalem, there will be
further changes in the topography of the land: "all the land will
be changed into a plain" (14:10). The Hebrew says literally, "all
the land will be changed as the Arabah." The Arabah is the low
land extending from Mount Hermon to the Red Sea. It is the
lowest point below sea level in the world and includes the Sea
of Galilee and the Dead Sea. Much of this area is fertile, and so
the promise is one of blessing on the land.

The extent of this area is from Geba to Rimmon, south of
Jerusalem. Geba is probably Gibea of Saul in Benjamin (Josh.
18:24). Rimmon is usually identified with the southern border of

the tribe of Judah (Josh. 15:32), as Geba is with the northern border.

The phrase "Jerusalem will rise and remain on its site" (14:10) refers to the restoration of the city. The city of Jerusalem in Zechariah's day was not a pretty sight. The rubble of the 586 B.C. destruction was all around, and the walls were not rebuilt until Nehemiah's time. This vision sees the city rebuilt in glory. The designation of the geographical points of the city ("from Benjamin's Gate as far as the place of the First Gate to the Corner Gate, and from the tower of Hananel to the king's wine presses") is probably an allusion to Jeremiah's prophecy of the rebuilding of Jerusalem (Jer. 31:38–40). Jeremiah says, " 'Behold, days are coming,' declares the LORD, 'when the city shall be rebuilt for the LORD from the Tower of Hananel to the Corner Gate.' " Jeremiah's promise is in the context of the New Covenant, which will be applied to Israel in the end times. The rebuilding of the city is included in that promise, and Zechariah links Jeremiah's prediction with his own.

The prosperity of the city is shown by the fact that people will live in it, and there will be no more curse (14:11). The word translated *curse* is a technical word used for a city or people who were placed under a "ban"—to be destroyed. Jericho was such a city (Josh. 6:18), and the Amalekites were such a people (1 Sam. 15:1–3). God promises that such a curse will not come upon Jerusalem. Jerusalem will dwell safely.

C. The Lord Punishes the Nations (14:12–15)

Now the prophecy addresses the nations who had the audacity to come against Jerusalem. This discussion was postponed to allow for elaboration on the blessing upon the remnant. The Lord is going to bring a devastating plague upon the nations as a part of His warfare against them. This unimaginable plague will destroy the nations, and great panic will come upon them (14:13). In that day men will fight one another. (There was a similar sequence of events in 1 Samuel 5:9, where confusion among the people followed the plague.)

When God fights on her side, Judah will take courage and fight in Jerusalem. Again there will be cooperation between Judah (the countryside) and Jerusalem (the city) as in chapter

12. The nations who were in the very act of despoiling
Jerusalem (14:1) will in turn be despoiled, and great wealth will
accrue to the Jews.

The plague will come upon the animals as well as on the
people (14:15). In warfare the animals carry equipment, men,
and supplies. The destruction of the animals indicates the
complete destruction of the Gentile powers.

D. The Blessing of the Lord (14:16–21)

The discussion of the king, begun in 14:9, is now resumed.
This section shows the impact of the king's rule on the nations.

1. The Remaining Nations Will Come to Jerusalem (14:16)

A common theme in Scripture is that Jerusalem will be the
center of the messianic rule on earth. The nations who survived
God's great destruction will come to Jerusalem to an annual
Festival of Booths to worship King Jehovah.

The New Testament interprets the typology of four of the
feasts of Israel (Lev. 23). The Passover was observed by the
Lord who then died as the Passover lamb. Paul says, "Christ our
passover [lamb] also has been sacrificed"(1 Cor. 5:7). He
continues, "Let us therefore celebrate the feast, not with old
leaven, nor with the leaven of malice and wickedness, but with
the unleavened bread of sincerity and truth." The second feast
was that of Unleavened Bread. It followed immediately after the
Passover and was celebrated for seven days. This, says Paul, is
the symbol of a holy life growing out of the death of the Paschal
Lamb. The Feast of the Firstfruits is related to the resurrection
of Christ in 1 Corinthians 15:23. It was during the Feast of the
Harvest (Pentecost), fifty days after the Resurrection, that the
Holy Spirit came down.

The three remaining feasts are Trumpets, Day of Atonement, and the Feast of Booths. In the Millennium, the nations
will come to Jerusalem to celebrate the Feast of Booths. This
festival was a time of rejoicing at the ingathering of the crops. It
was also to remind Israel of her sojourning in the wilderness
(Lev. 23:39–43). The returning exiles in Ezra's day kept the

Festival of Booths (Ezra 3:1–4). This Feast will also have special emphasis in the Millennium.

2. Disobedient Nations Will Be Punished (14:17–19)

Not all will be obedient during the Millennium (cf. Rev. 20:7–9); some will need divine persuasion. Any nations refusing to come to Jerusalem (tantamount to refusing allegiance to the Lord) will find their rain withheld. Egypt is singled out, possibly because they do not depend on rainfall as much as other nations (cf. 10:1–2 for a fuller discussion). In spite of their consistent water supply, God says He will bring a plague on Egypt or any other nation that refuses to come to Jerusalem to celebrate the Feast of Booths.

3. A Great Sense of Holiness (14:20–21)

These verses are written to demonstrate that the special presence of God in Jerusalem will bring a true sense of holiness upon the land. The bells on the horses will be inscribed with "Holy to the LORD" and the ringing phrase of the seraphim will be heard: "holy, holy, holy" (Isa. 6:3). Holiness will be so pervasive that even the common pots of the temple will be like sacrificial vessels before the altar. The common pots of the land will be considered holy, and people will use them as part of their sacrificial acts.

The last statement is very difficult. The Hebrew says, "There will not be a Canaanite any longer in the house of God." The word translated *Canaanite* also means "to be a merchant." There seems to be a negative connotation attached to the name. However, the meaning is clear enough: No unclean person will be in the temple—all will be holy.

E. Summary

The final section of the book (chaps. 12–14) shows Israel in the last days under great oppression, but delivered by God as they turn to Him in repentance. (The phrase "in that day" occurs in 12:3, 4, 6, 8 (twice) 9, 11; 13:1, 2, 4; 14:4, 6, 8, 9, 13, 20, 21.) This portion of the book is very important eschatologically and is referred to often in the New Testament. Israel will be attacked by a world confederacy, but she will have victory over that combined attack. The Spirit of the Lord will minister to the nation of Israel, and they will look on Him whom they have pierced. The messianic kingdom will be established, and God's people will be restored as a holy nation.

For Further Study

1. Read Matthew 24:15–31. When do you believe the nations will gather against Jerusalem?

2. Read Exodus 14:15–31. Is there any similarity between the Exodus account of God's deliverance and what He will do in the future?

3. Compare the contents of 14:4–8 with Revelation 12. What similarities do you see and what are the implications of those similarities?

4. Read 1 John 3:1–2. How should the teaching of chapter 14 affect you as a Christian?